The Buddhist Chef's
Vegan Comfort Cooking

The Buddhist Chef's
Vegan Comfort Cooking

EASY, FEEL-GOOD RECIPES FOR EVERY DAY

JEAN-PHILIPPE CYR

appetite
by RANDOM HOUSE

Appetite by Random House® and colophon are registered trademarks of Penguin Random House LLC.

Library and Archives Canada Cataloguing in Publication is available upon request.
ISBN: 978-0-525-61145-5
eBook ISBN: 978-0-525-61146-2

Photography © Samuel Joubert, except those on page 21, 26, 41, 42, 59, 60, 77, 85, 86, 96, 100, 109, 151, 199, 200, and 202, which are by Dominique Lafond
Translation by Marie Asselin
Printed and bound in China

Published in Canada by Appetite by Random House®, a division of Penguin Random House Canada Limited.

www.penguinrandomhouse.ca

10   9   8   7   6   5   4   3   2   1

TABLE OF CONTENTS

INTRODUCTION

When I was a child, my mother and grandmother made it their mission to make me as self-sufficient as possible. It was out of the question that I'd be "pampered and spoiled," as they put it. By the age of six, I was a feminist by proxy and they were training me to become the most helpful husband someday. I learned to cook standing on a small bench between these two passionate cooks. They had me cleaning pots and pans before I even had time to call for help. This was far from a punishment; as it happened, I loved spending time in the kitchen.

As I look back on my childhood, I realize how lucky I was to grow up in a time when the pleasure of cooking and eating was paramount. There was no online food delivery, and smartphones weren't at the kitchen table. Instead, we kids would hop on our bikes to go pick up strawberries or apples from the local stands or do a grocery run for our parents. What a time. While we would cook out of necessity, we would still enjoy preparing foods in the kitchen and eating together as a family, free from distraction. It was a time when we enjoyed getting seconds and thirds . . . without worrying about calories or fats. A lot has changed since then. We now live in a digital world and have access to information at our fingertips. We also have a better understanding of where our food comes from and how our dietary choices impact the planet.

As for me, I became a classically trained chef, a Buddhist, and a vegan, in that order. I used my culinary training to veganize meals. I launched The Buddhist Chef blog and have loved sharing my vegan creations with you online and in my first cookbook, *The Buddhist Chef*. It's been great to see all of you—whether you are trying to reduce your meat intake or are a long-time vegan—embrace these plant-based recipes.

I'm so excited to share even more vegan meals with you. These recipes are inspired by the nostalgic comfort foods I enjoyed growing up, as well as by popular foods from around the world. I hope they make veganism easy for you and your loved ones while bringing back memories of simpler times. Let me know what you think!

THE BUDDHIST CHEF PANTRY

My classic comfort food recipes celebrate timeless ingredients: vegetables and grains. But what if you are craving a traditional dish where dairy or meat is the star? How do you recreate those textures and flavors? Making veganized classics is so simple, you just need a few key ingredients to get you started and cook the recipes in this book.

PLANT-BASED PROTEINS

LEGUMES are edible seeds from fabaceous plants that are harvested from pods, such as lentils and chickpeas. Legumes have many benefits—in terms of nutrition, price, and environment—and because they're an excellent source of vegetable protein, fiber, iron, and vitamins, they are central to a balanced diet. On store shelves, you can find legumes in cans (already cooked) or dried. Use whichever you prefer, just be sure to soak dried legumes first. When you first start adding more fiber-rich lentils and beans to your diet, your body might need a bit of time to adjust.

MISO is a fermented paste made from fermenting soybeans with rice or other grains. Hailing from Japan, it has a salty and earthy flavor that adds depth to many dishes, including soups, broths, or marinades. The longer the fermentation, the darker in color and more flavorful it becomes. So, at your local grocery store, you'll find it comes in many colors, including white, yellow, and red. Any miso paste will do for these recipes.

TEMPEH is a vegetable protein made from whole soybeans, which gives it even more protein and fiber than tofu. Tempeh is fermented and has a more compact texture. It also has a more complex flavor full of umami, the famous fifth fundamental taste (in addition to sweet, sour, salty, and bitter). Tempeh is originally from Indonesia, where it is a staple used in many dishes, fresh or dried. It's very high in antioxidants and isoflavones, contains various B vitamins, and has natural antibiotic properties due to the mold used to ferment it. Tempeh also has lots of fiber, amino acids, high-quality protein, calcium, and essential fatty acids, and it is very low in fat.

TEXTURED VEGETABLE PROTEIN (TVP) is a dietary protein made from soy flour. When you rehydrate it, it can be a vegan substitute for ground meat.

TOFU is probably the protein that most people associate with a plant-based diet. It is made from soybean milk. Rich in protein and calcium and low in fat, tofu is very versatile and has a fairly neutral taste, which allows it to absorb the flavor of whatever you season it with. For savory dishes, I suggest getting the firmest tofu you can find. The labeling can be confusing, so verify the tofu by touch. Firm or extra-firm tofu should have the firmness of mozzarella cheese. Silken, a much softer form of tofu, is mainly used in creamier dishes and desserts.

PLANT-BASED DAIRY SOURCES

NUTRITIONAL YEAST is a type of inactive yeast, rich in B-complex vitamins, that is used as a condiment in vegan cooking. Why is it in the plant-based dairy sources section of this book? Because it adds a cheesy flavor. You can find it in stores in flake form. Don't confuse this with baker's yeast or brewer's yeast!

PLANT MILKS are milks made from cereals and grains. I like to use soy milk, but you can substitute your favorite plant milk (almond, cashew, etc.) in most of the recipes in this book. Make sure to always use unsweetened varieties.

VEGAN MAYONNAISE is a substitute for regular mayonnaise that doesn't contain eggs. It's made with soybean oils instead. Many popular brands, including traditional mayonnaise brands, make vegan versions nowadays and they are available at your local grocer.

GRAINS

BROWN SHORT-GRAIN RICE is a nutritious, fiber-rich type of whole-grain rice that contains the bran layer and cereal germ without the rice hull coating. It's delicious as a side dish, and I also like to use it to bind veggie burgers. It requires a longer cooking time than white rice, but soaking it beforehand will reduce the time it takes.

QUINOA is a high-protein whole grain rich in iron. It is excellent as a side dish or salad, among other uses. Cook it like rice in one and a half or two times its volume of water. Note that quinoa grains are covered with a slightly bitter coating (called saponin) that must be removed by rinsing the quinoa thoroughly with water before cooking.

VITAL WHEAT GLUTEN FLOUR is wheat flour with a high protein content. Gluten gives bread its elasticity, and gluten flour cannot be substituted with all-purpose or gluten-free flour. Gluten flour is used to make many things, like seitan, a vegan meat substitute.

OILS AND CONDIMENTS

LIQUID SMOKE is a water-soluble, natural condiment used in very small quantities. As its name suggests, it imparts a smoky flavor. You can usually find it in grocery stores near the barbecue sauce or you can order it online.

OLIVE OIL is a must-have ingredient that has a very distinctive flavor. Use extra-virgin for these recipes.

VEGAN BUTTER offers the rich taste of butter without dairy. Many brands are commercially available (made with different oils and proteins), such as Earth Balance, and they are available at your local grocer. Any will work for these recipes.

VEGETABLE OIL is a neutral-tasting oil, great for deep-frying. I like to use canola or sunflower oil.

BREAKFAST AND BRUNCH

Frittata

Serves 4 | **Prep Time: 25 min** | **Cook Time: 50 min**

Sometimes when I'm chatting with my wife, I get the impression she is distracted by other things. That is, until the moment I offer her a frittata. I then receive her undivided attention, and for good reason: this recipe is a marvel, as delicious for lunch or dinner as it is for breakfast.

Tofu Eggs:
1 (5½ oz/150 g) block firm tofu
2 cups (500 mL) plant milk
1 cup (125 g) all-purpose flour
¼ cup (30 g) cashews
3 tablespoons nutritional yeast
2 teaspoons maple syrup
1 teaspoon garlic powder
1 teaspoon dried basil
1 teaspoon dried oregano
1 teaspoon salt
⅛ teaspoon turmeric
Black pepper, to taste

Sautéed Vegetables:
3 tablespoons olive oil
4 cups (225 g) chopped
    mushrooms
12 broccoli florets, finely
    chopped
1 onion, chopped
2 yellow-fleshed potatoes
    (about 10½ oz/300 g),
    peeled and grated
1 cup (250 mL) vegetable broth
5 sun-dried tomatoes, chopped
1 teaspoon salt

1. Preheat the oven to 350°F (180°C).

For the Tofu Eggs:
2. Place all the ingredients in a blender. Blend until the mixture is smooth. Set aside.

For the Sautéed Vegetables:
3. In a skillet over medium-high heat, heat the oil. Add the mushrooms, broccoli, and onions and sauté, stirring occasionally, for 10 minutes.

4. Add the potatoes, broth, sun-dried tomatoes, and salt and keep cooking, stirring occasionally, for 5 to 7 minutes or until all the liquid is absorbed.

To Assemble:
5. If the skillet is ovenproof, pour the tofu mixture over the vegetables. Otherwise, transfer the vegetables to an ovenproof dish and mix in the tofu mixture.

6. Bake for 30 to 35 minutes or until golden. Serve.

Tofu Benedict

Serves 2 | **Prep Time: 40 min** | **Cook Time: 20 min**

As breakfast is the most important meal of the day, I often have it twice—you can never be too careful! You'll be back for seconds, too, after tasting this delicious tofu Benedict.

Hollandaise:
2 tablespoons all-purpose flour
2 tablespoons vegetable oil
1 cup + 2 tablespoons (280 mL) plant milk
3 tablespoons nutritional yeast
1 teaspoon garlic powder
1 teaspoon salt
1 teaspoon lemon juice
½ teaspoon maple syrup

Tofu Eggs:
1 (8 oz/225 g) block extra-firm tofu
2 cups (500 mL) vegetable broth
1½ tablespoons apple cider vinegar
1 teaspoon Himalayan salt or 2 teaspoons salt

Mushrooms:
1½ tablespoons vegetable oil
3 portobello mushrooms, sliced
4 cups (70 g) baby spinach
Salt and black pepper, to taste

For the Hollandaise:

1. In a saucepan over medium heat, whisk together the flour and oil for 1 to 2 minutes.

2. Add the milk. Whisking constantly, bring the mixture to a boil. Lower the heat to medium and whisk in the remaining ingredients until combined.

3. Keep cooking for 1 to 2 minutes, whisking constantly, until the sauce is smooth. Set aside.

For the Tofu Eggs:

4. Cut the tofu into 4 equal slices widthwise.

5. In a saucepan over high heat, bring the vegetable broth to a boil. Add the tofu, apple cider vinegar, and salt. Lower the heat to medium-low and simmer for 10 minutes.

6. Remove from the heat and let the tofu rest in the broth until ready to serve.

For the Mushrooms:

7. In a skillet over high heat, heat the oil, then add the mushrooms and sauté for 5 minutes.

8. Add the baby spinach, then season with salt and pepper and stir to combine. Set aside.

Recipe continues

Recipe continued

To Serve:
2 English muffins, halved and toasted
Handful of chives, minced
Orange wedges (optional)

To Serve:

9. Place 2 of the toasted English muffin halves on each plate.

10. Spoon the mushroom mixture over each English muffin half, then top each with a tofu egg.

11. If necessary, return the hollandaise to the heat for a few minutes to warm up. Cover the tofu eggs with the hollandaise sauce and garnish each with chives.

Scrambled White Beans with Breakfast Potatoes and Tempeh Sausages

Serves 4 | **Prep Time: 45 min** | **Cook Time: 1 hour**

When you adopt a vegan diet, finding something to eat for breakfast often becomes your greatest challenge—well, that and convincing some of your friends to come over for a plant-based brunch. But don't panic. Serve these fabulous scrambled white beans with a side of breakfast potatoes and tempeh sausages (or even baked tomatoes and mushroom caps), and even those picky eaters will thank you.

Breakfast Potatoes:
½ teaspoon baking soda
1 teaspoon salt, + more for seasoning
6 yellow-fleshed potatoes (about 2 lb/900 g)
¼ cup (60 mL) olive oil

Scrambled White Beans:
3 tablespoons vegetable oil
4 cups (70 g) baby spinach
6 mushrooms, minced
4 sun-dried tomatoes, chopped
1 clove garlic, minced
2 (19 oz/540 mL) cans white beans, rinsed and drained
2 tablespoons nutritional yeast
2 teaspoons maple syrup
½ teaspoon garlic powder
¼ teaspoon turmeric
Salt and black pepper, to taste
Water or vegetable broth (optional)

For the Breakfast Potatoes:
1. Preheat the oven to 375°F (190°C).

2. Fill a large pot with water. Place over high heat, stir in the baking soda and salt, and bring to a boil.

3. Peel the potatoes, then cut into cubes. Add the potatoes to the boiling water and cook for 10 minutes. Drain and let rest for 5 minutes.

4. In a large bowl, combine the potatoes with the oil, then season with salt. Toss to coat.

5. Spread the potatoes over a baking sheet.

6. Bake for 40 minutes, tossing the potatoes at the halfway mark. Season to taste when ready to serve. Meanwhile, make the scramble and sausages.

For the Scrambled White Beans:
7. In a skillet over medium-high heat, heat the oil, then add the baby spinach, mushrooms, sun-dried tomatoes, and garlic and cook, stirring, for 5 minutes.

Recipe continues

Recipe continued

Tempeh Sausages:

¼ cup + 2 tablespoons (90 mL) vegetable oil

1 (8½ oz/240 g) package tempeh, cut into sticks

¾ cup (180 mL) vegetable broth

1 tablespoon tomato paste

1 tablespoon maple syrup

2 teaspoons onion powder

1 teaspoon dried thyme

1 teaspoon paprika

1 teaspoon salt

½ teaspoon fennel seeds

½ teaspoon dry mustard

Pinch of cayenne pepper

8. Add the remaining ingredients and keep cooking for 5 minutes or until heated through.

9. Using a fork, roughly mash the mixture, adding a bit of water or vegetable broth to loosen if the mixture is too thick. Set aside.

For the Tempeh Sausages:

10. In a skillet over high heat, heat the oil, then add the tempeh sticks and cook for 5 minutes, turning them from time to time to brown evenly.

11. Add the remaining ingredients. Keep cooking until the liquids are fully absorbed.

12. Lower the heat to medium-high, then add more oil if needed and keep cooking for 3 minutes or until the sausages are brown and crisp.

To Serve:

13. Divide the scramble, potatoes, and tempeh sausages among the plates. Season to taste.

Vegan Cream Cheese

Makes 1 cup (250 mL) | **Prep Time: 15 min** | **Rest Time: 1 hour**

People often ask me whether I miss my cheese-eating days. The answer is no. Why? Because a plant-based alternative with herbs does the trick. This is best served with bagels.

½ cup (60 g) cashews
1 (8 oz/225 g) block silken tofu
½ cup (125 mL) vegetable oil
2 tablespoons minced chives
1 tablespoon apple cider vinegar
2 teaspoons garlic powder
1 teaspoon onion powder
1 teaspoon salt
½ teaspoon maple syrup
Bagels, for serving (optional)

1. Soak the cashews in boiling water for 10 minutes. Drain.

2. Place the cashews and remaining ingredients in a blender. Blend until the mixture is very smooth.

3. Pour the mixture into an airtight container and refrigerate to set for at least 1 hour before serving.

4. Enjoy as a spread for toasted bagels, or serve as desired. The vegan cream cheese will keep in an airtight container in the fridge for up to 5 days.

Apple and Cinnamon Oatmeal

Serves 4 | **Prep Time: 20 min** | **Cook Time: 25 min**

Do you think oatmeal is boring? Well, think again! Once you've tried it with my apple and cinnamon compote, oatmeal is going to become your new favorite breakfast—I promise. The compote is also excellent served cold with vegan yogurt or as a garnish for crêpes.

Oatmeal:
4½ cups (360 g) rolled oats
8 cups (2 L) plant milk
Pinch of salt

Apple and Cinnamon Compote:
4 apples, cored, peeled, and diced
½ cup (65 g) raisins
10 pitted dates (3½ oz/100 g), chopped
½ teaspoon ground cinnamon or 1 cinnamon stick
¼ to ½ cup (60 to 125 mL) water

Pumpkin seeds, to garnish

For the Oatmeal:

1. In a saucepan, combine the oats, milk, and salt. Bring to a boil, then simmer for 8 to 10 minutes. Set aside.

For the Apple and Cinnamon Compote:

2. In a saucepan, combine all the ingredients.

3. Set over medium-high heat and bring to a boil.

4. Lower the heat and simmer for 20 minutes, stirring frequently. Set aside. The compote will keep in an airtight container in the fridge for up to 5 days.

To Serve:

5. Discard the cinnamon stick, if using. Divide the oatmeal between the serving bowls.

6. Spoon some of the compote over each.

7. Sprinkle with pumpkin seeds and enjoy.

Zucchini Muffins with Pumpkin Seeds

Makes 12 muffins | **Prep Time: 30 min** | **Cook Time: 30 min**

No one will be able to resist these muffins. They're light and "not too sweet," as my mother would often say. I like them warm from the oven, but they're also excellent chilled. Enjoying a muffin and getting a dose of veggies all at once—what's not to like?

1 cup (220 g) packed brown
   sugar
½ cup (125 mL) vegetable oil
½ cup (125 mL) applesauce
½ cup (125 mL) plant milk
1 teaspoon lemon juice
2 cups (200 g) grated zucchini
2 cups (250 g) all-purpose flour
1 teaspoon baking powder
1 teaspoon baking soda
1 teaspoon salt
⅓ cup (50 g) pumpkin seeds

1. Preheat the oven to 350°F (180°C).

2. Line a 12-cup circular or rectangular muffin pan with paper cups or grease the cups thoroughly.

3. In a bowl, use a whisk or hand mixer to beat together the brown sugar, oil, applesauce, milk, and lemon juice until combined. Fold in the grated zucchini until incorporated. Set aside.

4. In a second bowl, whisk together the flour, baking powder, baking soda, and salt. Pour the wet ingredients over the dry ingredients and mix to combine.

5. Divide the batter between the prepared cups. Sprinkle with pumpkin seeds.

6. Bake for 30 minutes or until a toothpick inserted in the middle comes out clean.

7. Remove from the pan, let cool slightly on a wire rack, then enjoy. Leftovers can be kept in an airtight container at room temperature or in the fridge for up to 5 days.

French Toast with Caramelized Bananas and Maple Syrup

Serves 4 | **Prep Time: 15 min** | **Cook Time: 20 min**

When I was growing up, camping was a family tradition, much to the dismay of my mother, who vastly preferred sleeping somewhere warm and dry—what a concept! My father was in charge of breakfast when we camped, and French toast was his specialty—when he wasn't burning it! Here's some delicious French toast to enjoy, whether in the great outdoors or in the comfort of your own home.

French Toast:
2 cups (250 g) all-purpose flour
2 cups (500 mL) plant milk
½ cup (125 mL) maple syrup
2 tablespoons vegetable oil
1 teaspoon baking soda
1 teaspoon vanilla extract
Pinch of salt
8 slices crusty bread
½ cup (125 mL) vegan butter, divided

Caramelized Bananas:
½ cup (125 mL) maple syrup
4 bananas, sliced into rounds

For the French Toast:

1. Preheat the oven to 200°F (95°C). Place a baking dish in the oven large enough to hold the toast.

2. In a bowl, whisk together the flour, milk, maple syrup, oil, baking soda, vanilla extract, and salt.

3. Dip each slice of bread into the batter, piercing it with a fork a few times to allow it to soak up more of the batter.

4. In a skillet over medium-high heat, melt some of the vegan butter. Add 2 slices of bread and cook until both sides are golden brown, about 2 to 3 minutes per side. Place in the oven to keep warm until ready to serve. Repeat.

For the Caramelized Bananas:

5. In a skillet over high heat, bring the maple syrup to a boil and cook until slightly thickened, about 3 minutes.

6. Add the sliced bananas and cook for 3 to 4 minutes or until golden brown, flipping them halfway through.

To Serve:

7. Divide the French toast among the plates and top each with the caramelized bananas.

Breakfast Date Cookies

Makes 10 cookies | **Prep Time: 15 min** | **Cook Time: 15 min**

There isn't always time for a healthy breakfast. I created these breakfast date cookies for those busy mornings. These cookies will amaze you with their simplicity and rich flavor! They're also excellent as a snack or as a guilt-free dessert.

2½ cups (310 g) pitted dates

½ cup (125 mL) maple syrup, divided

¼ cup (60 mL) vegetable oil

1½ cups (190 g) all-purpose flour

1 cup (80 g) rolled oats

½ teaspoon ground ginger

½ teaspoon ground cinnamon

½ teaspoon salt

1. Preheat the oven to 400°F (200°C). Line a baking sheet with parchment paper.

2. Soak the dates in boiling water for 10 minutes. Drain.

3. Transfer the dates to a food processor. Add ¼ cup (60 mL) of the maple syrup and the oil and blend until smooth.

4. Add the flour, oats, ginger, cinnamon, and salt and blend until the dry ingredients are fully incorporated.

5. Divide the dough into 10 balls. Set the cookie balls on the prepared sheet.

6. Bake for 12 to 15 minutes, until cooked through.

7. Remove the cookies from the oven and immediately brush them with the remaining maple syrup to glaze them. Let sit for 15 minutes before serving. Cookies will keep in an airtight storage container at room temperature for about 4 days.

SOUPS AND SALADS

Cream of Mushroom and Spinach Soup

Serves 6 | **Prep Time: 20 min** | **Cook Time: 35 min**

Apparently, some people believe that soup is an older person's dish, but there is truly no age limit for loving soup! In fact, it's a delicious way to get little ones to appreciate vegetables, like this soup does with spinach.

Cashew Cream:
½ cup (125 mL) vegetable broth
¼ cup (30 g) cashews
2 tablespoons nutritional yeast
1 tablespoon vegetable oil
2 teaspoons maple syrup
1 teaspoon dried basil
1 teaspoon dried oregano
1 teaspoon garlic powder
1 teaspoon apple cider vinegar
1 teaspoon salt

Mushrooms:
3 tablespoons vegetable oil
8 cups (450 g) sliced
   mushrooms
2 onions, minced
6 cups (1.5 L) vegetable broth
4 cups (70 g) spinach
5 yellow-fleshed potatoes
   (about 25 oz/750 g), peeled
   and cut into cubes

To Serve:
2 tablespoons soy cream
   (optional)
Handful chives, chopped
   (optional)

For the Cashew Cream:
1. In a blender, combine all the ingredients until smooth. Set aside.

For the Mushrooms:
2. In a pot over medium-high heat, heat the oil, then add the mushrooms and onions and cook, stirring, for 5 minutes.

3. Add the vegetable broth, spinach, and potatoes.

4. Bring to a boil, lower the heat, and simmer for 30 minutes.

5. Stir in the cashew cream.

6. Using an immersion blender, or by transferring the mixture to a blender, blend until smooth.

To Serve:
7. Divide the soup among the bowls.

8. Swirl in soy cream and sprinkle with chives, if desired.

French Onion Soup

Serves 4 | Prep Time: 30 min | Cook Time: 55 min

It's time to dig out your onion soup bowls for this delicious vegan take on French onion soup.

3 tablespoons vegetable oil
6 cups (600 g) sliced onions
¾ cup (180 mL) dry white wine
6 cups (1.5 L) vegetable broth
¼ cup (60 mL) miso paste
2 bay leaves
1 teaspoon dried basil
1 teaspoon dried oregano
Salt, to taste
4 slices baguette, toasted
1 recipe Vegan Mozzarella
   (page 149)

1. In a large pot over medium-low heat, heat the oil, then add the onions and cook for 15 minutes, stirring from time to time, until tender.

2. Add the white wine, scrape the bottom of the pot to deglaze, then continue cooking until the mixture is reduced by half, about 3 minutes.

3. Add the vegetable broth, miso paste, bay leaves, basil, and oregano. Mix well.

4. Bring to a boil, then simmer over medium-high heat for 30 minutes. Season with salt to taste. Discard the bay leaves.

5. Set the oven to broil. Place 4 French onion soup bowls or ovenproof bowls over a baking sheet. Divide the soup between the bowls, then top each serving with a toasted baguette slice. Divide the vegan mozzarella among the bowls.

6. Broil for about 4 minutes or until the cheese is melted and golden brown.

Vegetable and White Bean Soup

Serves 6 to 8 | **Prep Time: 30 min** | **Cook Time: 1 hour, 10 min**

As a child, I was so tall that I often had to lie about my age; otherwise, people might have thought that my parents were giving me steroids. The real reason for my surprising height was much less controversial: vegetables. My mother would hide them everywhere and employed various tricks to make me eat them—hypnosis, emotional blackmail, and so on. I kid, of course.

3 tablespoons vegetable oil
½ head green cabbage (10 oz/ 280 g), minced
3 carrots, sliced into rounds
3 stalks celery, chopped
1 onion, chopped
8 cups (2 L) vegetable broth
1 (28 oz/796 mL) can diced tomatoes
1 (19 oz/540 mL) can white beans, rinsed and drained
2 yellow-fleshed potatoes (about 10½ oz/300 g), peeled and cut into cubes
3 bay leaves
1 teaspoon dried basil
1 teaspoon dried oregano
Salt and black pepper, to taste

1. In a large pot over medium heat, heat the oil, then add the cabbage, carrots, celery, and onions and cook, stirring, for 10 minutes.

2. Add the remaining ingredients, bring to a boil, lower the heat, cover, and simmer for 1 hour.

3. Discard the bay leaves, season to taste, and serve.

Split Pea Soup

Serves 6 to 8 | Prep Time: 20 min | Cook Time: 1 hour, 40 min

My grandmother raised so many children (16!) that there were two Roberts in the family. Children, grandchildren, friends, and strangers were constantly milling about the house, sometimes without her knowledge. What could be better to feed a huge table of hungry people than classic, hearty, warming split pea soup?

3 tablespoons vegetable oil
1 large onion, chopped
2 carrots, diced
2 stalks celery, diced
8 cups (2 L) vegetable broth
1½ cups (300 g) dried split peas
1 tablespoon miso paste (optional)
1 teaspoon salt
½ teaspoon dried savory
Black pepper, to taste

1. In a large pot over medium heat, heat the oil, then add the onions and cook, stirring, for 5 minutes.

2. Add the carrots and celery and keep cooking for 5 minutes, stirring constantly.

3. Add the vegetable broth, split peas, miso paste (if using), salt, and savory. Bring to a boil. Cover and simmer over low heat for about 90 minutes or until the peas are tender.

4. Season to taste with black pepper and serve.

Easy Tofu Noodle Soup

Serves 6 | **Prep Time: 15 min** | **Cook Time: 20 min**

Whenever I was sick as a little boy, my mother would make me chicken noodle soup. I was inspired by my mother's recipe to create this easy tofu version, which will be pleasing to both children and parents alike. Don't wait until you are sick to savor this comforting and tasty soup!

8 cups (2 L) vegetable broth

1 (19 oz/540 mL) can tomato juice

1 (12½ oz/350 g) block firm tofu, diced

1½ cups (120 g) dry soup noodles

1 cup (180 g) frozen mixed vegetables

¼ cup (15 g) nutritional yeast

1 tablespoon miso paste

2 bay leaves

1 teaspoon dried basil

1 teaspoon dried oregano

1 teaspoon garlic powder

1 teaspoon onion powder

½ teaspoon Tabasco sauce or hot sauce

¼ teaspoon dried sage

Salt and black pepper, to taste

1. In a large pot, combine all the ingredients.

2. Bring to a boil, lower the heat, cover, and simmer for 20 minutes.

3. Discard the bay leaves.

4. Season to taste and enjoy.

Hearts of Palm Bisque

Serves 8 | **Prep Time: 30 min** | **Cook Time: 50 min**

I love soups! They are such a tasty way to add more vegetables to our diet without even realizing it. Silky and ever-so-slightly spicy, the flavor of this hearts of palm soup will amaze you. Trust me, you will never look at hearts of palm the same way again!

3 tablespoons olive oil
2 carrots, diced
2 stalks celery, diced
1 yellow onion, chopped
6 cups (1.5 L) vegetable broth
2 (14 oz/398 mL) cans hearts of palm, rinsed and drained, and cut into rounds
3 yellow-fleshed potatoes (about 15 oz/450 g), peeled and diced
½ cup (60 g) cashews
1 teaspoon sambal oelek
1 teaspoon salt
½ teaspoon dried thyme
Black pepper, to taste

1. In a large saucepan over medium heat, heat the oil, then add the carrots, celery, and onions. Cook, stirring, for 6 to 7 minutes.

2. Add all the remaining ingredients. Stir to combine, then bring to a boil.

3. Lower the heat and simmer for 40 minutes.

4. Using a slotted spoon, scoop about 1½ cups (375 mL) of the solids from the soup. Set aside.

5. Use an immersion blender or a regular blender to blend the remaining soup until smooth.

6. Stir the solids back into the smooth soup and serve.

Corn Chowder

Serves 8 | **Prep Time: 20 min** | **Cook Time: 35 min**

This classic corn chowder is my wife's favorite soup—we eat it every week! And why not? It's simply delicious. The sweetness of corn adds a little extra something. I guarantee you'll make and enjoy this chowder again and again.

6 ears corn or 4 cups (660 g) frozen corn kernels

3 tablespoons vegetable oil

1 onion, chopped

6 cups (1.5 L) vegetable broth

3 large yellow-fleshed potatoes (about 15 oz/450 g), peeled and diced

1 cup (250 mL) soy cream (such as Belsoy)

3 tablespoons canned diced jalapeños (optional)

Salt, to taste

1. Shuck the corn, then use a sharp knife to cut the kernels off the cobs. Set the corn kernels aside. If using frozen corn, keep in the freezer until step 3.

2. In a saucepan over medium heat, heat the oil, then add the onions and cook, stirring, for 5 minutes.

3. Add the broth, potatoes, soy cream, jalapeños (if using), and fresh or frozen corn kernels.

4. Bring the mixture to a boil, lower the heat, and simmer for 30 minutes. Season to taste, and enjoy.

Spicy Noodle Soup

Serves 2 | **Prep Time: 20 min** | **Cook Time: 25 min**

Soups are like quiet weekends: the older you get, the more you appreciate them.

3 bok choy, halved or quartered

2 tablespoons vegetable oil

3 cups (195 g) minced Savoy cabbage

1 cup (60 g) sliced shiitake mushrooms

½ red bell pepper, sliced

2 shallots, minced

2 tablespoons minced ginger

2 cloves garlic, minced

1 (14 oz/398 mL) can coconut milk

1 cup (250 mL) vegetable broth

2 tablespoons red curry paste (adjust the quantity to taste)

1 tablespoon cane sugar

2 (3 oz/85 g) packages dry ramen noodles

1 (7 oz/200 g) block firm tofu, diced

Salt, to taste

1 chili pepper, chopped, to garnish (optional)

Lime wedges, for serving (optional)

1. Cook the bok choy in boiling water for 3 minutes. Drain and set aside.

2. In a saucepan over medium heat, heat the oil, then add the cabbage, shiitake mushrooms, bell peppers, shallots, ginger, and garlic and cook, stirring, until the vegetables are tender, about 10 minutes.

3. Add the coconut milk, vegetable broth, curry paste, and cane sugar and stir to combine. Bring to a boil, lower the heat, and simmer for about 10 minutes or until the vegetables are cooked through.

4. Add the ramen noodles, tofu, and bok choy.

5. Season to taste and serve immediately.

Caesar Salad with Tofu Chicken

Serves 4 | **Prep Time: 40 min** | **Cook Time: 25 min**

In the words of Julius Caesar: I came, I saw, I conquered . . . and I ate some tofu chicken Caesar salad!

Almond Bacon:
2 tablespoons nutritional yeast
2 tablespoons soy sauce
2 tablespoons liquid smoke
2 tablespoons maple syrup
1½ tablespoons vegetable oil
¾ cup (75 g) slivered almonds

Tofu Chicken:
1 (1 lb/450 g) block firm tofu
Salt
⅓ cup (40 g) cornstarch
2 tablespoons nutritional yeast
½ teaspoon dried sage
½ cup (125 mL) plant milk
¾ cup (90 g) breadcrumbs

For the Almond Bacon:

1. In a bowl, combine the nutritional yeast, soy sauce, liquid smoke, maple syrup, and oil.

2. Line a baking sheet with parchment paper.

3. In a skillet over medium-high heat, toast the almonds for 4 to 5 minutes, stirring constantly. Add the toasted almonds to the wet ingredients, stirring to coat.

4. Spread the almonds on the prepared sheet and let cool completely.

For the Tofu Chicken:

5. Preheat the oven to 375°F (190°C). Generously grease a baking sheet with oil.

6. Slice the tofu into sticks and season generously with salt. Set aside.

7. In a bowl, combine the cornstarch, nutritional yeast, and sage. Pour the milk into a second bowl and place the breadcrumbs in a third bowl. Dredge each tofu stick in the cornstarch mixture, then quickly dip into the milk, then coat with breadcrumbs.

8. Place the tofu sticks on the prepared sheet and bake for 15 to 20 minutes or until golden, flipping the sticks halfway through.

Recipe continues

Recipe continued

Dressing:

½ cup (125 mL) olive oil

¼ cup (60 mL) canola oil

3 tablespoons Dijon mustard

3 tablespoons drained capers, chopped

2 tablespoons maple syrup

1 tablespoon vegan Worcestershire sauce

1 teaspoon lemon juice

1 teaspoon Tabasco sauce or hot sauce

2 cloves garlic, minced

Salt and black pepper, to taste

Croutons:

3 tablespoons olive oil

½ baguette, cut into cubes

2 heads Romaine lettuce, whole or torn, for serving

For the Dressing:

9. Place all the ingredients in a bowl.

10. Using an immersion blender or whisk, blend until smooth. Set aside.

For the Croutons:

11. In a skillet over medium-high heat, heat the oil.

12. Add the baguette cubes and sauté for about 5 minutes or until the croutons are golden brown on all sides. Set aside.

To Serve:

13. Place the Romaine lettuce in a large bowl.

14. Add the dressing, tofu chicken, almond bacon, and croutons and toss to combine.

Tempeh Grain Bowls

Serves 2 | Prep Time: 20 min | Cook Time: 20 min

I love both grain and salad bowls. I put my yoga pants on and make myself a bowlful of veggies, grains, and protein—it's so healthy that sometimes I don't have to actually do yoga.

Maple-Glazed Tempeh:

1 (8½ oz/240 g) package
  tempeh, cubed
½ cup (125 mL) vegetable broth
3 tablespoons maple syrup
2 tablespoons toasted sesame oil
2 tablespoons soy sauce
1 tablespoon nutritional yeast
2 teaspoons sesame seeds
2 teaspoons liquid smoke
1 teaspoon garlic powder
1 teaspoon sambal oelek

Peanut Dressing:

¼ cup (60 mL) natural peanut
  butter
¼ cup (60 mL) vegetable oil
2 tablespoons soy sauce
2 tablespoons mirin
1 tablespoon maple syrup
Juice from 1 lime
1 teaspoon sambal oelek
Salt, to taste

Quinoa:

1 cup (170 g) quinoa, rinsed
2 cups (500 mL) water

For the Maple-Glazed Tempeh:

1. Combine all the ingredients in a saucepan.

2. Bring to a boil, lower the heat, and simmer for about 10 minutes or until the liquid is fully absorbed. Set aside.

For the Peanut Dressing:

3. Place all the ingredients in a bowl.

4. Using an immersion blender or a whisk, blend until combined. Set aside.

For the Quinoa:

5. In a saucepan, combine the quinoa and water.

6. Bring to a boil, cover, then reduce the heat and simmer for 10 minutes or until the liquid is fully absorbed.

7. Use a fork to fluff up the quinoa.

Recipe continues

Recipe continued

For Serving:

Romaine lettuce leaves, torn into large pieces

Handful of cherry tomatoes, halved

Handful of microgreens

1 recipe Toasted Tortilla Strips (page 54)

To Assemble:

8. Divide the lettuce between serving bowls.

9. Arrange the tempeh, quinoa, tomatoes, and tortilla strips over top. Enjoy with the peanut dressing.

Orzo and Chickpea Salad

Serves 4 | **Prep Time: 20 min** | **Cook Time: 10 min** | **Rest Time: 15 min**

What could be more romantic than a picnic, especially in the summertime with someone special? Munching on salad while sitting on the grass sounds delightful—no wonder rabbits always seem happy!

Citrus Dressing:

⅓ cup (80 mL) vegan mayonnaise
¼ cup (60 mL) olive oil
Zest and juice from ½ orange
Juice from 1 lime
2 tablespoons maple syrup
2 teaspoons minced ginger
2 teaspoons salt
1 teaspoon Tabasco sauce or hot sauce
Black pepper, to taste

Salad:

2 cups (380 g) dry orzo pasta
1 (19 oz/540 mL) can chickpeas, rinsed and drained
2 stalks celery, finely chopped
2 carrots, grated
4 green onions, minced
½ cup (65 g) raisins
¼ cup (15 g) chopped fresh parsley

For the Dressing:

1. Place all the ingredients in a bowl.

2. Using an immersion blender or regular blender, blend until smooth. Set aside.

For the Salad:

3. Cook the orzo pasta according to the package directions. Rinse under cold water, drain, and let cool.

4. Transfer the orzo to a salad bowl, then add the remaining ingredients and dressing.

5. Toss to combine, and serve.

Taco Salad with Jalapeño Dressing

Serves 4 | Prep Time: 30 min | Cook Time: 10 min

Be the star of the next potluck with this extraordinary salad. You might even be invited back—for a vegan, that's saying something!

Dressing:
¼ cup (60 mL) olive oil
3 tablespoons vegan mayonnaise
2 tablespoons chopped pickled jalapeños
2 tablespoons maple syrup
1 tablespoon apple cider vinegar
2 teaspoons pickled jalapeño liquid
1 teaspoon salt
Black pepper, to taste

Toasted Tortilla Strips:
2 tablespoons vegetable oil
2 large tortillas, cut into strips
Pinch of salt

Charred Corn:
1 cup (165 g) frozen corn kernels

Salad:
2 heads Romaine lettuce, sliced
15 cherry tomatoes, halved
½ red onion, minced
1 avocado, diced

For the Dressing:

1. In a bowl, whisk together all the dressing ingredients. Set aside.

For the Toasted Tortilla Strips:

2. In a large skillet over medium heat, heat the oil, then add the tortilla strips and cook for 5 minutes, tossing from time to time, until the strips are golden brown. Sprinkle with salt and set aside.

For the Charred Corn:

3. Set the oven to broil. Grease a baking sheet with oil.

4. Spread the corn over the baking sheet, then broil for about 4 minutes or until charred in spots. Set aside.

For the Salad:

5. Place all the salad ingredients in a large bowl.

6. Add the dressing and corn.

7. Toss to mix, then garnish with toasted tortilla strips. Serve immediately.

Greek Fusilli Salad

Serves 4 | Prep Time: 30 min | Cook Time: 10 min | Rest Time: 2 hours

If vegans only eat salad, as they say, it should be this one!

Tofu Feta:
1 (8 oz/225 g) block firm tofu
2 cloves garlic
1 tablespoon olive oil
2 teaspoons salt
1 teaspoon maple syrup
1 teaspoon dried oregano
1 teaspoon onion powder

Pasta:
9 oz (250 g) dry fusilli pasta

Dressing:
¾ cup (180 mL) vegan
    mayonnaise
½ English cucumber, diced
1 tablespoon chopped fresh dill
1 tablespoon maple syrup
2 teaspoons garlic powder
2 teaspoons apple cider vinegar
1 teaspoon dried oregano
1 teaspoon salt
Black pepper, to taste

To Serve:
10 cherry tomatoes, halved
½ red onion, minced
½ red bell pepper, chopped
2 cups (50 g) arugula

For the Tofu Feta:
1. Cut the tofu into a small dice.

2. Peel the garlic cloves and use a knife to smash them. Add the tofu, garlic, and the remaining ingredients to a jar. Cover with 1 cup (250 mL) of water. Close the lid and gently shake the jar to distribute the seasonings.

3. Place in the fridge and let marinate for at least 2 hours, and up to 1 week

For the Pasta:
4. Cook the pasta according to the package directions.

5. Rinse under cold water, drain, and set aside at room temperature.

For the Dressing:
6. Place all the ingredients in a bowl.

7. Use an immersion blender to combine. Set aside.

To Serve:
8. In a large bowl, toss the pasta with the tofu feta and dressing. Toss in the tomatoes, onions, bell peppers, and arugula, and serve.

Warm Lentil and Sweet Potato Salad

Serves 2 | Prep Time: 20 min | Cook Time: 30 min

Want to eat healthy without feeling like you're depriving yourself? Try this warm lentil and sweet potato salad. The sweet potatoes lend a little sweetness (naturally), and the lentils bring along their own specialty: protein. This salad will leave you feeling satisfied and energized.

2 sweet potatoes (1 lb/500 g)
4 tablespoons (60 mL) olive oil, divided
Salt and black pepper, to taste
2 tablespoons soy sauce
1 tablespoon maple syrup
1 tablespoon apple cider vinegar
1 tablespoon whole-grain mustard
3 cups (75 g) arugula
1 (14 oz/398 mL) can green lentils, rinsed and drained

1. Preheat the oven to 375°F (190°C). Grease a baking sheet with oil.

2. Peel and dice the sweet potatoes, then transfer to a bowl. Drizzle with 2 tablespoons of the olive oil, then season with salt and pepper.

3. Spread the seasoned sweet potato cubes on the prepared sheet, then bake for 30 minutes or until the sweet potatoes are tender and browned in spots. Set aside.

4. In a large bowl, whisk together the remaining olive oil, soy sauce, maple syrup, apple cider vinegar, and whole-grain mustard.

5. Add the arugula, lentils, and roasted sweet potatoes.

6. Toss to combine, and serve.

Roasted Sweet Potato and Chickpea Bowl

Serves 1 | Prep Time: 15 min | Cook Time: 30 min

Looking for the perfect protein-filled post-workout meal? Look no further. Peanut butter and chickpeas are both significant sources of protein, so dig in! It makes a perfect dinner for one (hence the serving), but can easily be doubled or tripled, so everyone can enjoy.

Roasted Sweet Potato:
1 small sweet potato, skin on
2 tablespoons olive oil
Salt or steak spice mix, to taste

Dressing:
2 tablespoons soy sauce
1 tablespoon peanut butter
1 tablespoon maple syrup
1 tablespoon balsamic vinegar

To Serve:
2 leaves lettuce, torn
1 cup (160 g) cooked Brown Rice (page 101)
½ cup (125 mL) canned chickpeas, rinsed and drained
¼ red onion, thinly sliced
1 tomato, sliced
½ avocado, sliced

For the Roasted Sweet Potato:

1. Preheat the oven to 375°F (190°C). Generously grease a baking sheet with oil.

2. Slice the sweet potato in half lengthwise.

3. Season the sweet potato halves with salt or steak spice, then place them cut side down on the baking sheet.

4. Bake for 20 to 30 minutes. Set aside.

For the Dressing:

5. Place all the dressing ingredients in a bowl.

6. Use an immersion blender or whisk to combine.

To Serve:

7. Lay the lettuce leaves in the bottom of a bowl.

8. Add the brown rice, then the baked sweet potatoes, chickpeas, sliced tomatoes, and avocados.

9. Drizzle with the dressing and enjoy.

APPETIZERS AND SIDES

Tomato Fritters

Serves 2 to 4 | Prep Time: 15 min | Cook Time: 18 min | Rest Time: 15 min

I was traveling in Greece when I discovered these little fritters, called *tomatokeftedes*. They are so perfect that you'll wonder why they aren't more popular here. Serve with a glass of white wine and make sure to have sunscreen handy.

Tzatziki Mayonnaise:
- ¾ cup (180 mL) vegan mayonnaise
- 2 tablespoons chopped fresh dill, + more to garnish
- ½ teaspoon onion powder
- ½ English cucumber with the peel on, chopped or grated

Fritters:
- 3 tomatoes, diced
- ½ red onion, minced
- ¼ cup (15 g) chopped fresh parsley, + more to garnish
- ½ teaspoon ground cumin
- ½ teaspoon dried oregano
- ½ teaspoon salt
- ¼ teaspoon red pepper flakes
- ¾ cup (90 g) all-purpose flour
- Olive oil, for frying

For the Tzatziki Mayonnaise:

1. In a bowl, combine all the ingredients.

2. Chill in the fridge until ready to serve.

For the Fritters:

3. In a large bowl, combine the tomatoes, onions, parsley, cumin, oregano, salt, and red pepper flakes.

4. Use your hands to mash all the ingredients together.

5. Add the flour and mix to combine. Adjust the flour quantity if needed; the mixture should remain slightly loose.

6. Let the mixture rest for 15 minutes.

7. Divide the mixture into ¼-cup (60 mL) portions, then flatten into fritters.

8. In a skillet, heat 2 to 3 tablespoons of olive oil. In batches if necessary, cook the fritters until they're golden brown and cooked through, about 3 minutes on each side. Add oil between batches as needed.

9. Serve with the tzatziki mayonnaise and a sprinkle of chopped dill and parsley.

Onion Bhajis

Serves 4 | **Prep Time: 20 min** | **Cook Time: 12 min** | **Rest Time: 1 hour**

Onion bhajis are delicious fritter-style snacks originally from India, and these are my version. They're great for gatherings. Just prepare the dough in advance and fry up these bite-size portions when guests arrive. They are best served with spicy sweet-and-sour sauce, like my spicy red pepper sauce.

Bhajis:
6 onions (1½ lb/675 g), minced
1 cup (120 g) chickpea flour
½ cup (60 g) all-purpose flour
6 tablespoons (90 mL) water
2 teaspoons ground cumin
2 teaspoons salt
1 teaspoon turmeric
½ teaspoon red pepper flakes
Black pepper, to taste

Spicy Red Pepper Sauce:
½ cup (100 g) cane sugar
½ cup (125 mL) water
1 tablespoon rice vinegar
1 tablespoon tomato paste
1 clove garlic, minced
¼ teaspoon red pepper flakes
1 tablespoon cornstarch
1 tablespoon water

Vegetable oil, for frying

For the Bhajis:
1. In a large bowl, combine all the ingredients.
2. Let the batter rest for 1 hour in the fridge.

For the Spicy Red Pepper Sauce:
3. In a saucepan, combine the sugar, water, rice vinegar, tomato paste, garlic, and red pepper flakes. Bring to a boil, lower the heat, and simmer for 10 minutes.
4. In a small bowl, combine the cornstarch with the water.
5. Add the cornstarch mixture to the saucepan and stir to combine.
6. Bring to a boil while stirring constantly. Keep cooking for 1 minute.
7. Remove from the heat and set aside at room temperature.

To Serve:
8. In a large pot or deep fryer, add enough oil to cover the bhajis and heat the oil to 350°F (180°C).
9. Drop 1 spoonful of the bhaji mixture into the oil at a time, making sure the bhajis are not touching each other or overcrowded.
10. Fry the bhajis in batches for 2 to 3 minutes, then turn them and keep cooking for 2 minutes more or until golden brown.
11. Serve with the spicy red pepper sauce.

No-Crab Cakes

Makes 8 cakes | **Prep Time: 30 min** | **Cook Time: 35 min** | **Rest Time: 1 hour**

When I was a child, we often vacationed on the east coast of the United States. These trips inspired me to reinvent the classic crab cake by replacing the crab with hearts of palm. The texture is just like the original and the taste is even better, in my opinion. These no-crab cakes are delicious whether eaten immediately or reheated the next day.

3 tablespoons vegetable oil

2 (14 oz/398 mL) cans hearts of palm, drained and cut into rounds

1 small onion, chopped

½ red bell pepper, chopped

1 stalk celery, chopped

1¼ cups (135 g) breadcrumbs

¼ cup (30 g) all-purpose flour

3 tablespoons nutritional yeast

3 tablespoons maple syrup

1 sheet nori, torn into pieces

1 teaspoon Dijon mustard

1 teaspoon onion powder

1 teaspoon garlic powder

1 teaspoon salt

½ teaspoon celery salt

½ teaspoon smoked paprika

½ teaspoon lemon juice

Tomato Sauce (page 150), for serving

1. In a large skillet over medium-high heat, heat the oil, then add the hearts of palm, onions, bell peppers, and celery and cook, stirring, for 7 minutes.

2. Add the remaining ingredients and keep cooking for 5 minutes.

3. Refrigerate the mixture for at least 1 hour.

4. Preheat the oven to 375°F (190°C). Grease a baking sheet with oil.

5. Shape the mixture into 8 small, flattened cakes.

6. Transfer the cakes to the prepared sheet. Bake for 20 minutes, flipping the cakes at the halfway mark.

7. Serve with the tomato sauce.

Lentil-Stuffed Buns

Makes 12 buns | **Prep Time: 30 min** | **Cook Time: 20 min**

Remember those party invitations where the hosts would ask you to bring your own dish AND a folding chair? Those potlucks were the best. I'll never forget Lucie's famous potato salad, Jean-Claude's macaroni salad, Micheline with her dip. Why do potlucks always taste better when served on a paper plate? Bring these lentil-stuffed buns to your next potluck and you're guaranteed to get invited back again and again. Just don't forget your chair.

3 tablespoons vegetable oil
4 cups (225 g) chopped mushrooms
2 carrots, grated
2 stalks celery, diced
1 green bell pepper, chopped
1 onion, chopped
2 (19 oz/540 mL) cans green lentils, rinsed and drained
½ cup (125 mL) vegetable broth
¼ cup (60 mL) ketchup
¼ cup (15 g) nutritional yeast
3 tablespoons soy sauce
3 tablespoons maple syrup
2 teaspoons yellow mustard
2 teaspoons chili spice mix
2 teaspoons liquid smoke
1 clove garlic, minced
Salt and black pepper, to taste
12 small buns, sliced, for serving

1. In a saucepan over medium heat, heat the oil, then add the mushrooms, carrots, celery, bell peppers, and onions and cook, stirring, for 10 minutes.

2. Add the remaining ingredients, except the buns, and keep cooking over medium-high heat for 10 minutes.

3. Use an immersion blender or transfer the mixture to a food processer to coarsely grind the mixture (optional).

4. To serve, fill each bun with the lentil mixture.

Stuffed Portobellos

Serves 2 | Prep Time: 20 min | Cook Time: 10 min

I hate recipes that require you to search to the ends of the earth to find the ingredients you need. Here's an easy dish for you—with readily available ingredients—that is oh so delicious.

Chipotle Mayonnaise:

¼ cup (60 mL) vegan mayonnaise
1 tablespoon ketchup
1 teaspoon maple syrup
Pinch of ground chipotle
Salt and black pepper, to taste

Roasted Mushrooms:

4 small or medium portobello mushrooms
2 tablespoons olive oil
2 teaspoons steak spice mix
Salt, to taste

Vegetable Topping:

1 avocado, diced
5 cherry tomatoes, halved
½ red onion, minced
Chopped fresh parsley, to garnish

For the Chipotle Mayonnaise:

1. In a bowl, combine the mayonnaise, ketchup, maple syrup, chipotle, and salt and pepper. Set aside if serving right away, or chill in the fridge for up to 1 week.

For the Roasted Mushrooms:

2. Preheat the oven to 400°F (200°C). Grease a baking sheet with oil.

3. Remove the stems from the portobello mushrooms. Set the mushrooms, top side down, on the prepared sheet. Brush with olive oil, then sprinkle with steak spice and season with salt.

4. Bake for 10 minutes. Set aside.

For the Vegetable Topping:

5. In a small bowl, place the avocados, tomatoes, and onions.

6. Add the chipotle mayonnaise and toss gently to combine. Set aside.

To Serve:

7. Place the warm roasted portobellos on a plate.

8. Top with the dressed vegetables and garnish with the chopped parsley.

Leek Rolls

Makes 9 rolls | Prep Time: 40 min | Cook Time: 45 min | Rest Time: 30 min

Brioche is my favorite dessert. In fact, I like it so much that I created a savory version with one of my favorite vegetables: leeks. Leeks are sweeter and subtler in flavor than onions. Plus, they go wonderfully with this delicious, creamy sauce made with cashews. Serve this to your guests and keep me posted—I bet it'll be a hit!

Pizza Dough:
- 1 cup (250 mL) warm water
- 1 (¼ oz/8 g) packet active dry yeast
- 1 tablespoon granulated sugar
- 2¼ cups (280 g) all-purpose flour
- 1 teaspoon salt

Cream Sauce:
- ⅓ cup (40 g) cashews
- 1 cup (250 mL) vegetable broth
- ⅓ cup (20 g) nutritional yeast
- 2 tablespoons cornstarch
- 2 tablespoons vegetable oil
- 1 tablespoon maple syrup
- 1 teaspoon apple cider vinegar
- ½ teaspoon garlic powder
- ½ teaspoon onion powder
- ½ teaspoon salt

For the Pizza Dough:

1. In a measuring cup or bowl, combine the warm water, yeast, and sugar. Let rest until the mixture foams, about 5 minutes.

2. In a large bowl, combine the flour and salt. Add the yeast mixture and stir to combine.

3. Cover the bowl with a clean, damp cloth. Let the dough rise for 30 minutes in a warm, draft-free spot.

4. Transfer the dough to a floured work surface, then knead for 2 to 3 minutes. Sprinkle with more flour to prevent the dough from sticking. Set aside.

For the Cream Sauce:

5. Soak the cashews in boiling water for 10 minutes. Drain.

6. In a blender, combine the cashews with the remaining ingredients and blend until creamy.

7. Transfer the mixture to a saucepan. Set over medium heat and bring to a boil while whisking constantly.

8. Once the sauce boils, keep cooking and whisking for about 2 minutes or until the mixture thickens. Set aside.

Recipe continues

Recipe continued

Filling:

3 tablespoons olive oil
1 large leek, minced
1 teaspoon salt
8 cups (140 g) baby spinach
½ cup (125 mL) dry white wine
2 cloves garlic, minced
1 teaspoon maple syrup
½ teaspoon truffle oil (optional)

For the Filling:

9. In a skillet over medium heat, heat the oil, then add the leeks, season with the salt, and cook, stirring from time to time, for 5 minutes.

10. Add the remaining ingredients and keep cooking for 5 minutes. Set aside.

To Assemble:

11. Preheat the oven to 375°F (190°C). Grease a 8 × 16-inch (20 × 40 cm) baking dish with oil.

12. Using a rolling pin, roll out the dough to create a 12 × 24-inch (30 × 60 cm) rectangle.

13. Spread the cream sauce all over the dough, making sure to leave a 1-inch (2.5 cm) border all around.

14. Scatter the leek mixture over the sauce. Roll up the dough, starting from the longer side. Cut into 9 equal portions.

15. Arrange the rolls snuggly side by side in the baking dish.

16. Bake for 25 minutes or until the tops are golden.

Provençal Crostini

Serves 4 | Prep Time: 30 min | Cook Time: 55 min

I discovered crostini on a trip to New York, where I was exploring the most popular vegan restaurants, always in search of inspiration. I fell in love with these pan-grilled toasts and their endless variety of toppings. Here, I chose to prepare the crostini *à la provençale*, incorporating sun-dried tomatoes and mixed herbs.

Roasted Garlic:
1 bulb garlic
1 tablespoon olive oil
Salt

Sautéed Vegetables:
3 tablespoons olive oil
1½ cups (120 g) minced leeks
1 red bell pepper, chopped
1 zucchini, diced
⅓ cup (45 g) slivered almonds
8 sun-dried tomatoes, chopped
1 tablespoon tomato paste
1 tablespoon maple syrup
2 cloves garlic, minced
1 teaspoon herbes de provence
1 teaspoon salt
Black pepper, to taste

For Serving:
1 tablespoon olive oil
2 thick slices crusty bread
Handful of basil leaves

For the Roasted Garlic:

1. Preheat the oven to 350°F (180°C).

2. Cut off the top of the garlic bulb and discard. Brush the exposed top lightly with oil, season with salt, and wrap in aluminum foil.

3. Bake for 45 minutes. Let cool.

For the Sautéed Vegetables:

4. In a skillet over medium-high heat, heat the oil, then add the leeks, bell peppers, zucchini, almonds, and sun-dried tomatoes and sauté for 10 minutes.

5. Add the remaining ingredients and keep cooking for 5 minutes. Set aside.

To Serve:

6. In a skillet over medium-high heat, heat the oil, then add the slices of bread and toast for 2 to 3 minutes per side, until golden brown.

7. Press 1 roasted garlic clove to extract its flesh over 1 crostini, then use a knife to spread it all over. Repeat with the second crostini.

8. Slice each crostini in two, then garnish with the sautéed vegetables and basil.

Vegan Cheese Fondue

Serves 4 | Prep Time: 15 min | Cook Time: 10 min

Through my efforts to adapt dairy recipes to vegan recipes, I made the delightful discovery that cashews can be used to create extraordinary plant-based cheeses. Here, I grind down the cashews and add white wine to recreate the typical taste of cheese fondue. And believe me, the taste will fool anyone!

⅓ cup (40 g) cashews
1½ cups (375 mL) plant milk
⅓ cup (80 mL) dry white wine
¼ cup (15 g) nutritional yeast
3 tablespoons tapioca starch
3 tablespoons vegetable oil
2 teaspoons maple syrup
1 teaspoon salt
½ teaspoon garlic powder
1 baguette, cubed, for serving

1. Soak the cashews in boiling water for 10 minutes. Drain.

2. In a blender, combine the soaked cashews with the remaining ingredients and blend until creamy.

3. Transfer the mixture to a saucepan. Set over medium heat and bring to a boil while whisking constantly. Once the sauce boils, keep cooking and whisk for 3 minutes.

4. Remove from the heat and serve the fondue, in a fondue pot if you have it, with sliced baguette.

Marinated Tofu

Makes 1 (16 oz/475 mL) jar | **Prep Time: 10 min** | **Rest Time: 24 hours**

Some things never go out of style, like leather pants or eggs in vinegar. I wanted to pay homage to the latter by creating "tofu in vinegar," a briny, marinated tofu you can snack on or eat in a salad.

1 (1 lb/450 g) block extra-firm tofu, sliced into cubes
¾ cup (180 mL) white vinegar
2 cloves garlic, peeled and smashed
2 tablespoons maple syrup
2 Thai peppers, sliced into thirds
¼ red onion, sliced
2 teaspoons salt

1. Combine all the ingredients in a jar and cover with water.

2. Close the lid and swirl to evenly distribute the seasonings.

3. Refrigerate for at least 24 hours before serving. The marinated tofu will keep in the fridge for up to 5 days.

Herbed New Potatoes

Serves 4 | **Prep Time: 10 min** | **Cook Time: 35 min**

I love potatoes. Thank goodness for that, as they're often the only thing a vegan like me can eat at certain restaurants. But you don't have to be vegan to enjoy these new potatoes. I guarantee success with this dish, vegan or not!

3 tablespoons vegetable oil
1 onion, minced
1½ lb (700 g) new potatoes
1 cup (250 mL) vegetable broth
1 teaspoon dried oregano
1 teaspoon dried basil
1 teaspoon salt
1 teaspoon maple syrup

1. Preheat the oven to 375°F (190°C).

2. In a large saucepan over medium-high heat, heat the oil, then add the onions and cook, stirring, for 5 minutes.

3. Add the remaining ingredients and bring the mixture to a boil.

4. If the saucepan is ovenproof, place in the oven. Otherwise, transfer the mixture to a baking dish.

5. Bake for 30 minutes or until the potatoes are tender and most of the liquid is absorbed. Serve. Potatoes will keep in an airtight container in the fridge for up to 5 days.

Braised Red Cabbage

Serves 4 | **Prep Time: 10 min** | **Cook Time: 1 hour to 1 hour, 30 min**

When I was a restaurant chef, I often prepared braised red cabbage, a staple of French cuisine. It makes an excellent side dish and brings remarkable color to the plate. This recipe is probably the tastiest way to highlight the magnificent vegetable that is cabbage.

¼ cup (60 mL) olive oil

8 cups (800 g) chopped red cabbage

¼ cup (60 mL) apple cider vinegar

3 tablespoons maple syrup

1 teaspoon salt

1. Preheat the oven to 325°F (160°C).

2. In a baking dish, combine all the ingredients and mix to ensure the cabbage is coated.

3. Bake for 1 hour to 1 hour and 30 minutes, or until the cabbage is tender.

Roasted Root Vegetables

Serves 4 | Prep Time: 10 min | Cook Time: 30 min

How do you enhance the flavor of root vegetables? By roasting them in the oven! You'll see, it works wonders.

4 yellow-fleshed potatoes (about 20 oz/600 g), quartered
4 carrots, sliced lengthwise
1 red onion, quartered
3 cloves garlic, peeled and smashed
¼ cup (60 mL) olive oil
2 teaspoons steak spice mix
½ teaspoon garlic powder
½ teaspoon onion powder
Salt, to taste

1. Preheat the oven to 400°F (200°C). Grease a baking sheet with oil.

2. In a bowl, combine all the ingredients.

3. Spread the vegetables on the prepared sheet.

4. Bake for 30 minutes, flipping the vegetables halfway through. Enjoy.

Roasted Cauliflower

Serves 2 to 4 as a side | **Prep Time: 10 min** | **Cook Time: 15 min**

Some people think that the purpose of cauliflower is to make other foods shine. I prefer to believe it enhances the dishes it goes with. This recipe will make you fall in love with cauliflower and appreciate it for what it is.

1 head cauliflower (2 lb/900 g), cut into florets
3 tablespoons vegetable oil
1 tablespoon maple syrup
1 teaspoon curry powder
½ teaspoon salt
¼ teaspoon turmeric
¼ teaspoon paprika

1. Preheat the oven to 400°F (200°C). Grease a baking sheet with oil.

2. In a bowl, toss the cauliflower florets with the remaining ingredients.

3. Spread the seasoned cauliflower on the prepared sheet.

4. Bake for 15 minutes, until browned.

Creamy Cauliflower and Spinach Casserole

Serves 4 | **Prep Time: 30 min** | **Cook Time: 40 min**

There are some things you learn to appreciate with age . . . cauliflower, tea, and ignoring a phone call come to mind. This recipe is one of my mother's classics—which I have, of course, "veganized," but let's keep that between us.

½ cup (60 g) cashews
2 cups (500 mL) vegetable broth
½ cup (60 g) nutritional yeast
¼ cup (60 mL) vegetable oil
2 tablespoons cornstarch
1 tablespoon maple syrup
2 teaspoons apple cider vinegar
1 teaspoon salt
1 head cauliflower (2 lb/900 g),
  cut into florets
8 cups (140 g) baby spinach
1 cup (130 g) frozen peas
½ cup (60 g) breadcrumbs

1. Preheat the oven to 350°F (180°C).

2. Soak the cashews in boiling water for 10 minutes. Drain.

3. In a blender, combine the cashews with the vegetable broth, nutritional yeast, oil, cornstarch, maple syrup, apple cider vinegar, and salt and blend until smooth.

4. Transfer the mixture to a saucepan. Set over medium heat and bring to a boil while whisking constantly.

5. Once the sauce simmers, keep cooking and whisk for about 2 minutes or until the mixture thickens. Set aside.

6. In a large saucepan, bring water to a boil, then add the cauliflower florets. Cook for 3 minutes. Drain.

7. Return the cauliflower to the pot and add the spinach and peas.

8. Add the sauce and stir well.

9. Transfer the mixture to a baking dish and sprinkle with the breadcrumbs.

10. Bake for 30 minutes or until the top is golden. Enjoy.

Gratin Dauphinois

Serves 4 | **Prep Time: 30 min** | **Cook Time: 40 min**

Gratin Dauphinois is a traditional French dish made with potatoes, milk, cream, and Gruyère cheese. This vegan version is a perfect and sophisticated dish to bring to your next potluck.

2 tablespoons olive oil
1 cup (80 g) minced leeks
1 cup (250 mL) vegetable broth
1 cup (250 mL) soy cream
2 tablespoons nutritional yeast
2 teaspoons salt
1 teaspoon maple syrup
Pinch of ground nutmeg
6 yellow-fleshed potatoes
   (about 2 lb/900 g)

1. Preheat the oven to 350°F (180°C).

2. In a saucepan over medium heat, heat the oil, then add the leeks and cook, stirring, for 5 minutes.

3. Add the vegetable broth, soy cream, nutritional yeast, salt, maple syrup, and nutmeg and stir to combine. Turn up the heat to medium-high and bring the mixture to a boil. Once it starts boiling, remove from the heat and set aside.

4. Using a mandoline or a sharp knife, thinly slice the potatoes.

5. Transfer the sliced potatoes to a baking dish.

6. Pour the cream sauce over the potatoes and bake for 30 to 40 minutes or until the potatoes are tender.

Grilled Mexican Corn on the Cob

Makes 8 ears of corn | Prep Time: 20 min | Cook Time: 15 min

Elote (aka grilled Mexican corn on the cob) is a street food that is very popular in Mexico and the United States. It's often served on a stick, but not always. Easy to prepare, it will help you rediscover fresh corn, which has a way-too-short season. After tasting corn on the cob dressed like this, I bet you'll wonder why you ever ate it any other way.

Corn:
8 ears of corn, shucked

Sauce:
⅓ cup (80 mL) vegan mayonnaise
¼ cup (60 mL) soy cream
⅓ cup (45 g) finely chopped cashews
1 teaspoon maple syrup
1 tablespoon lime juice
1 tablespoon nutritional yeast
1 teaspoon garlic powder
½ teaspoon dried oregano
¼ teaspoon ground chipotle
¼ teaspoon salt
¼ cup (35 g) finely chopped red onions, divided

Black pepper, to taste
Paprika, to taste
Sprigs of parsley, to garnish
Lime wedges, to garnish

For the Corn:

1. Preheat the barbecue to 450°F (220°C).

2. Set the corn directly on the grill. Grill for 12 to 15 minutes or until golden brown, rotating the corn frequently to grill evenly.

For the Sauce:

3. In a bowl, whisk to combine the mayo, soy cream, cashews, maple syrup, lime juice, nutritional yeast, garlic powder, oregano, chipotle, and salt.

4. Mix in half of the onions and reserve the other half for garnish. Set the sauce aside.

To Serve:

5. Slather the corn with the sauce, garnish with the remaining red onions, and sprinkle with black pepper and paprika to taste.

ENTREES

French Canadian "Meatball" Stew

Serves 4 to 6, makes 20 meatballs | Prep Time: 40 min |
Cook Time: 1 hour, 30 min | Rest Time: 2 to 24 hours

These meatballs, known as *ragoût de boulettes*, are a French Canadian classic. Here is my vegan interpretation, which is as delicious and hearty as ever. You can prepare and cook the meatballs in advance and store them in the fridge. All that's left to do is warm them up in their sauce before serving them.

Brown Rice:

1 cup (185 g) brown short-grain rice

Tofu Meatballs:

¼ cup (60 mL) vegetable oil
1 teaspoon salt
4 cups (225 g) chopped mushrooms
3 stalks celery, chopped
2 onions, minced
1 (19 oz/540 mL) can green lentils, rinsed and drained
½ cup (125 mL) dry white wine
2 tablespoons miso paste
2 tablespoons maple syrup
2 teaspoons tourtière spice mix or ¼ teaspoon ground cloves
1 teaspoon dried oregano
1 teaspoon dried basil
1 cup (120 g) breadcrumbs
½ cup (64 g) all-purpose flour
2 flax eggs (see note)
Salt and black pepper, to taste

For the Brown Rice:

1. Thoroughly rinse the rice under cold water.

2. Place the rice in a heavy-bottomed saucepan, then add 2½ cups (625 mL) of water. Bring to a boil, lower the heat to the minimum, cover, and simmer for 30 minutes or until the liquid is fully absorbed.

3. Remove from the heat and let rest, covered, for 20 minutes.

4. Refrigerate for at least 2 hours. This recipe will produce the 2½ cups (400 g) cooked rice needed in the tofu meatballs.

For the Tofu Meatballs:

5. In a large heavy-bottomed skillet over medium heat, heat the oil and add the salt. Then add the mushrooms, celery, and onions and cook, stirring, for 15 minutes.

6. Add the lentils, white wine, miso paste, maple syrup, tourtière spice, oregano, and basil and stir to combine. Keep cooking for 10 minutes over medium heat, stirring constantly. Taste and adjust seasoning, if needed.

7. Transfer the mixture to a large bowl, then add the 2½ cups (500 g) of cooked brown rice, breadcrumbs, flour, and flax eggs. Mix well.

Recipe continues

Recipe continued

Gravy:

¼ cup (60 mL) vegan butter
¼ cup (32 g) all-purpose flour
3 cups (750 mL) vegetable broth
¼ cup (15 g) nutritional yeast
2 tablespoons miso paste
2 tablespoons tomato paste
2 tablespoons soy sauce
1 tablespoon maple syrup
1 teaspoon onion powder
Black pepper, to taste

8. In a food processor, blend half of the mixture for 2 minutes. Transfer the blended mixture back into the bowl and mix back into the remaining, textured mixture to combine. Refrigerate for 2 to 24 hours.

9. Use a small ice-cream scoop to divide and shape the mixture into 20 balls. At this stage, you can refrigerate the tofu meatballs for up to 3 days, or you can freeze them. Just set them up on a lined baking sheet 1 inch (2.5 cm) apart and freeze for 1 hour before placing in an airtight container.

10. When ready to bake, preheat the oven to 350°F (180°C). Grease a baking sheet with oil.

11. Place the tofu meatballs, evenly spaced, on the prepared sheet and bake for 15 to 20 minutes until browned. Meanwhile, make the gravy.

For the Gravy:

12. In a saucepan, melt the vegan butter. Add the flour and whisk for 2 minutes.

13. Whisk in the broth, then bring to a boil while whisking constantly.

14. Add the remaining ingredients and keep cooking for 15 minutes, stirring regularly.

To Serve:

15. Divide the tofu meatballs among the plates and top with gravy.

Note: One flax egg is 1 tablespoon ground flaxseed combined with 2 tablespoons water. Just let it rest for a few minutes to thicken.

BBQ Tofu Burgers

Makes 4 burgers | **Prep Time: 30 min** | **Cook Time: 40 min**

Just because you cut back on meat doesn't mean you have to say goodbye to burgers. At your next barbecue, enjoy these tofu burgers. Who says eating vegan can't be decadent?

Patties:
- 2 tablespoons olive oil
- 1 zucchini, grated
- 2 shallots, minced
- 2 cloves garlic, minced
- 1 (8 oz/225 g) block firm tofu
- 3 sun-dried tomatoes, chopped
- 3 tablespoons quick-cooking oats
- ¼ cup (35 g) gluten flour
- 3 tablespoons breadcrumbs
- 3 tablespoons nutritional yeast
- 1 teaspoon herbes de provence
- 1 teaspoon balsamic vinegar
- ½ teaspoon dry mustard
- ½ teaspoon poultry seasoning
- ½ teaspoon salt

For the Patties:

1. Preheat the oven to 350°F (180°C). Grease a baking sheet with oil.

2. In a skillet over medium-high heat, heat the oil, then add the grated zucchini, shallots, and garlic and cook, stirring, for 5 minutes.

3. Transfer the mixture to a food processor. Add the remaining ingredients and blend for 2 to 3 minutes until the mixture can be shaped (it shouldn't be too smooth).

4. Shape the mixture into 4 patties. At this stage, you can refrigerate, covered, for up to 3 days, or you can freeze them. To freeze, just set them up on a lined baking sheet 1 inch (2.5 cm) apart and freeze for 1 hour before placing in an airtight container.

5. When ready to cook, in a skillet over medium-high heat, warm a little oil, then fry the patties for 4 minutes, carefully flipping them over halfway through.

6. Transfer the patties to the prepared sheet and bake for 20 minutes, flipping them halfway through. While the patties are cooking, make the barbecue sauce.

Recipe continues

Recipe continued

Barbecue Sauce:

½ **cup (125 mL) vegetable broth**
¼ **cup (60 mL) ketchup**
¼ **cup (60 mL) maple syrup**
3 **tablespoons soy sauce**
2 **teaspoons liquid smoke**
1 **teaspoon onion powder**
¼ **teaspoon red pepper flakes**
2 **teaspoons cornstarch mixed
into 1 tablespoon water**

4 **hamburger buns, for serving**

For the Barbecue Sauce:

7. In a saucepan, combine the vegetable broth, ketchup, maple syrup, soy sauce, liquid smoke, onion powder, and red pepper flakes.

8. Bring to a boil, lower the heat to medium, then simmer for 5 minutes.

9. Whisk in the cornstarch mixture.

10. Bring to a boil and keep cooking for 1 minute, whisking constantly. Set aside. The sauce will keep in the fridge for up to 5 days.

To Serve:

11. Butterfly the hamburger buns, place on an aluminum plate, and place in the oven for a few minutes until warmed.

12. Coat the patties in barbecue sauce right before serving.

13. Fill each bun with a patty and add your favorite condiments and toppings.

Tempeh Burgers

Makes 6 burgers | Prep Time: 30 min | Cook Time: 40 min

One American company is making a big splash with the Impossible Burger, a plant-based burger patty that tastes like real meat. I've had the opportunity to taste it a few times and let me tell you, the illusion is perfect. Here is my version of this popular patty.

Patties:

1 (8½ oz/240 g) package tempeh

4 cups (225 g) chopped mushrooms

1 large yellow onion, quartered

3 tablespoons olive oil

1 cup (200 g) cooked Brown Rice (page 101), cooled

¼ cup (15 g) nutritional yeast

3 tablespoons ketchup

2 tablespoons miso paste

2 tablespoons natural peanut butter

1 tablespoon maple syrup

1 teaspoon onion powder

1 teaspoon salt

1 teaspoon liquid smoke

1 cup (130 g) gluten flour

For the Patties:

1. Preheat the oven to 350°F (180°C). Grease a baking sheet with oil.

2. In a food processor, pulse the tempeh, mushrooms, and onions to chop.

3. In a skillet over medium-high heat, heat the oil, then add the tempeh mixture and cook, stirring, for 10 minutes.

4. Return the tempeh mixture to the food processor, then add the rice, nutritional yeast, ketchup, miso paste, peanut butter, maple syrup, onion powder, salt, and liquid smoke. Blend for 1 minute.

5. Transfer the mixture to a bowl, add the gluten flour, and knead for 2 to 3 minutes.

6. Shape the mixture into 6 patties. At this stage you can refrigerate, covered, for up to 3 days, or you can freeze them. To freeze, just set them up on a lined baking sheet 1 inch (2.5 cm) apart and freeze for 1 hour before placing in an airtight container.

7. When ready to bake, place the patties on the prepared sheet and bake for 30 minutes, flipping the patties halfway through. While the patties are baking, make the sriracha mayo. Once the patties are cooked, keep the oven on for the buns.

Recipe continues

Recipe continued

Sriracha Mayo:

⅓ **cup (80 mL) vegan mayonnaise**

1 teaspoon sriracha sauce

1 teaspoon maple syrup

½ **teaspoon lemon juice**

Salt, to taste

6 hamburger buns, for serving

For the Sriracha Mayo:

8. In a bowl, combine all the ingredients.

9. Set aside, or chill in the fridge for up to 5 days.

To Serve:

10. Butterfly the hamburger buns, place on an aluminum plate, and place in the oven for a few minutes until warmed.

11. To assemble, fill each bun with a patty, spread with sriracha mayo, and add your favorite condiments and toppings.

Ribs-Style Tempeh

Serves 2 | **Prep Time: 20 min** | **Cook Time: 15 min**

I have moved a lot. In fact, when I was a kid, my parents would move to a new neighborhood every two years! Each new home felt the same, but different. It was hard at the time, but now I know how to deal with change, move like a pro, and make new friends wherever I go. To this day, though, the hardest thing for me to pack is the kitchen. My pantry and fridge are always full of delicious herbs, spices, and sauces . . . like bottles and bottles of soy sauce. I love soy sauce! It's a great condiment that can add so much flavor to a dish, like how it transforms tempeh into these delicious plant-based ribs. This is great served with a small side salad and fries.

½ cup (125 mL) vegetable broth
¼ cup (60 mL) soy sauce
¼ cup (60 mL) ketchup
¼ cup (60 mL) maple syrup
2 teaspoons liquid smoke
1 teaspoon onion powder
¼ teaspoon red pepper flakes
1 (8½ oz/240 g) package
  tempeh

1. In a skillet or small saucepan, combine the broth, soy sauce, ketchup, maple syrup, liquid smoke, onion powder, and red pepper flakes. Bring to a boil, then add the whole tempeh.

2. Lower the heat, and simmer the mixture until it has thickened, about 10 minutes, flipping the tempeh from time to time to ensure even cooking.

3. Remove the tempeh from the sauce. Slice the tempeh into sticks, add to the sauce, and cook for a few minutes, stirring until coated.

4. Transfer the tempeh ribs to a serving dish. Brush the tempeh ribs with more of the sauce before serving.

Vegan Philly Cheesesteak Sandwich

Serves 4 | Prep Time: 30 min | Cook Time: 30 min

There's no need to go all the way to Philadelphia to enjoy a cheesesteak sandwich. In fact, you don't even need meat . . . or cheese. This dish lets you do your part for the environment while feasting!

"Cheese" Sauce:

⅓ cup (40 g) cashews
1 cup (250 mL) vegetable broth
¼ cup (15 g) nutritional yeast
1½ tablespoons cornstarch
1 tablespoon tomato paste
1 tablespoon maple syrup
2 teaspoons apple cider vinegar
½ teaspoon garlic powder
½ teaspoon onion powder
½ teaspoon salt

Tofu Steak:

¼ cup (60 mL) vegetable oil
4 cups (225 g) sliced mushrooms
1 red bell pepper, sliced
1 red onion, minced
1 (1 lb/450 g) block extra-firm tofu, thinly sliced
2 cloves garlic, minced
2 tablespoons vegan Worcestershire sauce
2 tablespoons maple syrup
2 teaspoons liquid smoke
2 teaspoons steak spice mix
Salt, to taste

4 hoagie rolls, for serving

For the "Cheese" Sauce:

1. Soak the cashews in boiling water for 10 minutes.

2. In a blender, combine the soaked cashews with the remaining ingredients and blend until creamy.

3. Transfer the mixture to a saucepan, set over medium-high heat, and bring to a boil while whisking constantly.

4. Let the sauce boil for 2 minutes. Set aside.

For the Tofu Steak:

5. Preheat the oven to 350°F (180°C).

6. In a saucepan over high heat, heat the oil, then add the mushrooms, bell peppers, and onions and sauté for 7 minutes.

7. Add the tofu and garlic and keep cooking for 2 minutes.

8. Add the remaining ingredients, mix gently to combine, then keep cooking for 5 minutes.

To Serve:

9. Halve the rolls and fill each with the tofu steak and the cheese sauce.

10. Toast the sandwiches for 10 minutes in the oven.

Homemade Vegan Hamburger Helper

Serves 4 | **Prep Time: 30 min** | **Cook Time: 25 min**

Thanks to this recipe, you will no longer have to worry about the neighbors judging you for feeding your children Hamburger Helper.

"Cheese" Sauce:
½ cup (60 g) cashews
1½ cups (375 mL) vegetable broth
⅓ cup (20 g) nutritional yeast
3 tablespoons vegetable oil
2 tablespoons cornstarch
1 teaspoon garlic powder
1 teaspoon onion powder
1 teaspoon apple cider vinegar

Tempeh Stir-Fry:
1 (8½ oz/240 g) package tempeh
3 tablespoons vegetable oil
1 green bell pepper, diced
1 onion, chopped
1 (14 oz/398 mL) can diced tomatoes
3 tablespoons ketchup
2 tablespoons maple syrup
2 teaspoons liquid smoke
2 cloves garlic, minced
1½ teaspoons salt
1 teaspoon dried basil
1 teaspoon dried oregano
¼ teaspoon red pepper flakes
Black pepper, to taste

4½ cups (350 g) cavatappi pasta

For the "Cheese" Sauce:
1. Soak the cashews in boiling water for 5 minutes. Drain.

2. In a blender, combine the soaked cashews with the remaining ingredients and blend until creamy.

3. Pour the mixture in a saucepan and bring to a boil, whisking constantly.

4. Once the mixture boils, lower the heat, simmer for 2 minutes, remove from the heat, and set aside.

For the Tempeh Stir-Fry:
5. Coarsely chop the tempeh, then crumble it using your hands.

6. In a saucepan over medium-high heat, heat the oil, then add the crumbled tempeh, bell peppers, and onions and cook, stirring, for 5 minutes.

7. Add the remaining ingredients, stir well, and keep cooking for 10 minutes.

8. Stir in the cheese sauce. Set aside.

To Serve:
9. Cook the pasta according to the package directions. Drain.

10. Return the pasta to the pot, then add the tempeh mixture and the sauce and stir to combine.

11. Reheat over low heat and serve.

Tempeh Chili with Rice

Serves 4 | **Prep Time: 30 min** | **Cook Time: 25 min**

Made with tempeh, this will be a hit at your next chili cook-off.

Tempeh Chili:
1 (8½ oz/240 g) package tempeh
½ cup (125 mL) vegetable broth
¼ cup (60 mL) vegetable oil
2 tablespoons ketchup
1 tablespoon nutritional yeast
2 teaspoons maple syrup
2 teaspoons liquid smoke
2 cloves garlic, minced
1 teaspoon chili powder
½ teaspoon salt

Rice:
2 tablespoons vegetable oil
1 zucchini, sliced into rounds
1 red bell pepper, diced
1 onion, chopped
1 jalapeño pepper, seeded and
    minced
1 (14 oz/398 mL) can black
    beans, rinsed and drained
2 cups (500 mL) vegetable broth
¾ cup (145 g) basmati rice,
    rinsed and drained
3 tablespoons tomato paste
1 tablespoon chili powder
1 teaspoon ground cumin
1 teaspoon maple syrup
1 teaspoon salt
1 clove garlic, minced

For the Tempeh Chili:
1. Coarsely chop the tempeh, then crumble it using your hands.

2. Transfer the crumbled tempeh and all the remaining ingredients to a skillet. Stir to combine.

3. Set over medium-high heat and cook until the liquid is fully absorbed, about 5 to 10 minutes.

For the Rice:
4. In a saucepan over high heat, heat the oil, then add the zucchini, bell peppers, onions, and jalapeño peppers and sauté for 5 minutes.

5. Add the remaining ingredients, bring to a boil, lower the heat, cover, and simmer for 12 minutes.

6. Remove from the heat, let rest for a few minutes, then serve with the tempeh chili.

Burrito Bowls

Serves 2 | **Prep Time: 30 min** | **Cook Time: 30 min**

Bored with sandwiches? Try the burrito bowl, which is like a burrito in a bowl!

Dressing:
⅓ cup (80 mL) olive oil
2 tablespoons spicy sauce
2 tablespoons lime juice
2 tablespoons maple syrup
Salt and black pepper, to taste

Rice:
1 cup (190 g) basmati rice
1½ cups (375 mL) water
2 tablespoons tomato paste
2 teaspoons chili powder
1 teaspoon ground cumin
½ teaspoon salt

Black Bean Puree:
2 tablespoons vegetable oil
1 onion, chopped
1 (19 oz/540 mL) can black
    beans, rinsed and drained
¾ cup (180 mL) vegetable broth
1 clove garlic, minced
½ teaspoon salt

To Serve:
1 head Romaine lettuce, chopped
15 cherry tomatoes, halved
1 avocado, quartered
¼ red onion, sliced
2 cups (55 g) corn tortilla chips

For the Dressing:
1. In a small bowl, combine all the ingredients. Set aside.

For the Rice:
2. Rinse the rice under cold running water, then transfer to a saucepan.

3. Add the remaining ingredients, bring to a boil, lower the heat, cover, and simmer for 8 to 10 minutes or until the liquid is fully absorbed.

4. Remove from the heat and let rest, covered, for at least 5 minutes.

For the Black Bean Puree:
5. In a saucepan over medium heat, heat the oil, then add the onions and cook, stirring, for 5 minutes.

6. Add the remaining ingredients, bring to a boil, lower the heat, cover, and simmer until the liquid is fully absorbed, about 5 minutes.

7. Transfer to a bowl and use an immersion blender to puree. Set aside.

8. Reheat the black bean puree before serving.

To Serve:
9. Divide the rice and Romaine lettuce between 2 bowls.

10. Top with the black bean puree, cherry tomatoes, avocados, and red onions, and drizzle with the dressing. Enjoy with tortilla chips.

Tofu Fajitas

Serves 4 | Prep Time: 30 min | Cook Time: 10 min

I'm a fan of dishes that are intended to be placed in the center of the table so that everyone can serve themselves family style. Sharing, preferably with people you know and love, greatly improves any meal.

Filling:
¼ cup (60 mL) vegetable oil
3 portobello mushrooms, sliced
1 red bell pepper, sliced
1 red onion, sliced
1 (12½ oz/350 g) block firm tofu, cut into sticks
2 cloves garlic, minced
1 tablespoon tomato paste
1 tablespoon maple syrup
1 teaspoon ground cumin
1 teaspoon smoked paprika
½ teaspoon celery salt
¼ teaspoon cayenne pepper
Salt and black pepper, to taste

Chipotle Mayonnaise:
¼ cup (60 mL) vegan mayonnaise
2 teaspoons maple syrup
¼ teaspoon lemon juice
Pinch of ground chipotle
Salt and black pepper, to taste

For Serving:
4 large tortillas
2 tomatoes, halved and sliced
Handful of lettuce, chopped

For the Filling:
1. In a skillet over high heat, heat the oil, then add the mushrooms, bell peppers, and onions and sauté for 5 minutes.

2. Add the tofu and garlic and keep cooking for 3 minutes.

3. Add the remaining ingredients and keep cooking for 2 minutes.

For the Chipotle Mayonnaise:
4. In a bowl, combine all the mayonnaise ingredients. Set aside.

To Serve:
5. Divide the filling between the 4 tortillas.

6. Garnish with tomatoes, lettuce, and chipotle mayonnaise.

7. Fold in half.

Tofu Ham
with Pineapple

Serves 4 | **Prep Time: 15 min** | **Cook Time: 20 min** | **Rest Time: 1 to 24 hours**

Baked ham with pineapple rings reminds us of days gone by. This unique classic is even better when made with tofu.

Marinade:

¼ cup (60 mL) soy sauce
¼ cup (60 mL) maple syrup
2 tablespoons vegetable oil
1 tablespoon liquid smoke
1 teaspoon onion powder
4 whole cloves
½ teaspoon mustard seeds

Tofu Ham:

1 (1 lb/450 g) block firm tofu
8 slices canned pineapple
8 maraschino cherries, stems
   removed

For the Marinade:

1. Combine all the marinade ingredients in a bowl. Set aside.

For the Tofu Ham:

2. Cut the tofu into 8 square slices. Place the tofu slices in a container with a tight-fitting lid and cover with the marinade.

3. Marinate in the fridge, covered, for at least 1 hour and up to 24 hours, flipping the container from time to time to allow all sides of the tofu to soak in the marinade.

4. Preheat the oven to 350°F (180°C).

5. In a baking dish, place a tofu square, layer with a pineapple slice, and place a cherry in the hole of each pineapple slice. Repeat, slightly layering the tofu over the edge of the previous square. Pour any marinade remaining in the container over the tofu and pineapple.

6. Bake for 20 minutes, frequently brushing the tofu slices with the marinade during baking.

7. Enjoy.

Harissa Tofu

Serves 4 | **Prep Time: 30 min** | **Cook Time: 30 min**

Want to spice up your life? Try harissa paste, a red pepper puree from Tunisia available at most grocery stores. It pairs nicely with tofu such as in this recipe, inspired by North African cuisine.

Toasted Almonds:
½ cup (50 g) slivered almonds

Coated Tofu:
¼ cup (30 g) cornstarch
2 tablespoons nutritional yeast
1 teaspoon ground cumin
1 teaspoon salt
1 (1 lb/450 g) block extra-firm tofu, cubed
3 tablespoons vegetable oil

Sauce:
¾ cup (100 g) raisins
3 tablespoons vegetable oil
1 zucchini, sliced into rounds
½ red bell pepper, sliced
2 shallots, minced
2 cloves garlic, minced
2 cups (500 mL) tomato coulis
5 sun-dried tomatoes, chopped
3 tablespoons brown sugar
1 tablespoon harissa paste
1 teaspoon ground cumin
1 teaspoon salt
Black pepper, to taste

For the Toasted Almonds:

1. Set the oven to broil.

2. Spread the slivered almonds on a baking sheet. Broil for 2 to 3 minutes or until golden brown. Set aside.

For the Breaded Tofu:

3. In a bowl, combine the cornstarch, nutritional yeast, cumin, and salt. Add the tofu and toss to coat with the seasonings.

4. In a skillet over medium-high heat, heat the oil, then add the tofu and cook for 10 to 12 minutes, stirring frequently. Set aside.

For the Sauce:

5. Soak the raisins in boiling water for 5 minutes. Drain and set aside.

6. In a skillet over medium-high heat, heat the oil, then add the zucchini, bell peppers, shallots, and garlic and cook, stirring, for 5 minutes.

7. Add the soaked raisins along with the remaining ingredients and stir to combine. Bring to a boil, lower the heat, and simmer for 15 minutes. If the sauce becomes too thick, whisk in a bit of water or vegetable broth. Remove from the heat.

8. Stir in the breaded tofu.

1½ cups (375 mL) vegetable broth
1½ cups (270 g) couscous
Handful fresh parsley leaves
Lemon wedges

To Serve:

9. If you are making couscous, in a saucepan, bring the vegetable broth to a boil. Remove from the heat and stir in the couscous. Cover and let rest for 5 minutes. Use a fork to fluff up the couscous.

10. Transfer the harissa tofu to the plates and scatter the toasted almonds over top. Sprinkle with parsley leaves Serve with the couscous, if using, and lemon wedges.

Hawaiian-Style Tofu

Serves 4 | **Prep Time: 30 min** | **Cook Time: 30 min**

My old neighbors had a Hawaiian tiki-style bar in the basement that made you feel like you were somewhere tropical. Enjoy this tofu, made with a sweet and tangy Hawaiian-style sauce, whether you have a tiki bar or not.

Tofu:
1 (1 lb/450 g) block firm tofu
¼ cup (30 g) cornstarch
3 tablespoons vegetable oil
⅓ cup (45 g) chopped cashews

Sauce:
2 tablespoons toasted sesame oil
1 tablespoon vegetable oil
½ red bell pepper, sliced
1 onion, minced
2 teaspoons minced ginger
2 cloves garlic, chopped
¼ head cauliflower (8 oz/225 g), cut into florets
1 (14 oz/398 mL) can pineapple chunks, drained
1 cup (250 mL) pineapple juice
½ cup (125 mL) vegetable broth
3 tablespoons cane sugar
2 tablespoons tomato paste
1 tablespoon soy sauce
2 teaspoons sambal oelek
2 teaspoons cornstarch
1 tablespoon water
Salt and black pepper, to taste

Cooked rice, for serving (optional)

For the Tofu:
1. Slice the tofu into cubes, then toss with the cornstarch. Line a plate with a paper towel.

2. In a skillet, heat the oil, then sauté half of the tofu cubes until they're golden brown. Transfer the tofu cubes to the prepared plate.

3. Sauté the remaining tofu cubes, adding the cashews toward the end of cooking to toast them slightly. Add more oil if needed. Set aside.

For the Sauce:
4. In a saucepan over medium heat, heat the toasted sesame and vegetable oils, then add the peppers and onions and cook, stirring, for 5 minutes.

5. Add the ginger and garlic and keep cooking for 2 minutes, stirring constantly.

6. Add the cauliflower, pineapple chunks, pineapple juice, vegetable broth, sugar, tomato paste, soy sauce, and sambal oelek and stir to combine. Keep cooking for 15 minutes.

7. In a small bowl, combine the cornstarch with the water. Whisk the cornstarch mixture into the sauce.

8. Bring to a boil, stirring continuously until the sauce thickens.

9. Add the tofu, stir well, adjust seasoning if needed, then serve with rice, if desired.

Maple and Mustard Tofu

Serves 4 | Prep Time: 30 min | Cook Time: 30 min

The sugar shack: a place to collect maple water to be boiled into a syrup. It's also where you can watch the kids run in circles thanks to their sugar high. But once you take the maple syrup home, it is a wonderful addition to many sweet and savory dishes, like this one.

Tofu:
¼ cup (30 g) cornstarch
2 tablespoons nutritional yeast
1 teaspoon dried sage
1 teaspoon herbes de provence
1 teaspoon salt
1 (1 lb/450 g) block firm tofu, sliced into cubes

Sauce:
3 tablespoons olive oil
2 shallots, minced
3 tablespoons cognac
½ cup (125 mL) vegetable broth
3 tablespoons maple syrup
2 tablespoons nutritional yeast
2 tablespoons whole-grain mustard
1 tablespoon Dijon mustard
Salt and black pepper, to taste

To Serve:
1 lb (450 g) green beans
2 tablespoons olive oil
Salt and black pepper, to taste
Potato Puree (page 174), for serving

For the Tofu:

1. Preheat the oven to 375°F (190°C). Grease a baking sheet with oil.

2. In a bowl, combine the cornstarch, nutritional yeast, sage, herbes de provence, and salt.

3. Add the tofu cubes and toss to coat with the seasonings.

4. Spread the tofu on the prepared sheet. Bake for 20 minutes, flipping the tofu cubes at the halfway mark. Set aside.

For the Sauce:

5. In a saucepan over medium heat, heat the oil, then add the shallots and cook, stirring, for 3 minutes.

6. Add the cognac and keep cooking for 2 minutes over high heat.

7. Add the remaining ingredients, stir well, lower the heat, and keep simmering for 5 minutes.

8. Add the tofu to the sauce and stir to coat.

To Serve:

9. Bring a pot of water to a boil. Add the green beans, and boil until tender, a few minutes. Drain, and toss the green beans with oil and season with salt and pepper.

10. Sprinkle the potato puree with the chives.

11. Serve the tofu with the potato puree and green beans.

Panang-Inspired Tofu

Serves 4 | **Prep Time: 30 min** | **Cook Time: 30 min**

My curiosity led me to explore extraordinary cuisines like this one, inspired by my trip to Thailand.

Tofu:
- 1 (1 lb/450 g) block extra-firm tofu
- ¼ cup (30 g) cornstarch
- ½ teaspoon salt
- 3 tablespoons vegetable oil

Sauce:
- ½ head cauliflower (1 Lb/450 g)
- 3 tablespoons vegetable oil
- ½ red bell pepper, chopped
- 2 shallots, minced
- 1 stalk lemongrass
- 3 fresh mint leaves, minced
- 2 cloves garlic, minced
- 4 cups (70 g) baby spinach
- 1 cup (250 mL) coconut milk
- 1 cup (250 mL) vegetable broth
- 3 tablespoons packed brown sugar
- 2 tablespoons peanut butter
- 2 tablespoons minced ginger
- Juice from ½ lime
- 2 tablespoons soy sauce
- 1 tablespoon + 2 teaspoons red curry paste
- ¼ teaspoon red pepper flakes
- Salt and black pepper, to taste
- 1 Thai pepper, chopped, to garnish (optional)

For the Tofu:
1. Cut the tofu into sticks, then dredge in the cornstarch and season generously with salt.

2. In a skillet over medium-high heat, heat the oil, then sauté half of the tofu sticks until they're golden brown, about 10 minutes.

3. Transfer the tofu sticks to a paper towel–lined plate.

4. Dredge and sauté the remaining tofu sticks, adding more oil to the pan if needed. Transfer to the prepared plate.

For the Sauce:
5. Cut the cauliflower into florets. Set aside.

6. In a skillet over medium-high heat, heat the oil, then add the peppers and shallots and cook, stirring, for 5 minutes.

7. Remove the tough outer leaves of the lemongrass. Bruise the lemongrass with the back of a knife, or smash with a mortar and pestle to release its aromas. Add the lemongrass to the skillet along with the cauliflower and remaining ingredients. Bring to a boil, lower the heat, and simmer for 10 minutes.

8. Add the fried tofu sticks to the sauce and stir to coat. Discard the lemongrass and serve.

Dengaku Tofu

Dengaku is a Japanese miso-glazed dish with sweet and savory flavors. The glaze is typically used with eggplant or tofu, and I have adapted it to a marinade. Sometimes the best recipes are the simplest!

Marinade:

¼ cup (60 mL) miso paste

¼ cup (60 mL) maple syrup

1 tablespoon mirin

1 teaspoon sambal oelek

1 tablespoon toasted sesame oil

1 (1 lb/450 g) block extra-firm tofu, sliced

1. Combine all the marinade ingredients in a bowl. Add the tofu and toss to coat with the marinade. Refrigerate for at least 1 hour and up to 24 hours.

2. When ready to serve, preheat the oven to 375°F (190°C) and grease a baking sheet with oil.

3. Transfer the tofu slices to the baking sheet. Bake for 20 minutes. Enjoy.

Cauliflower and Chickpea Curry

Serves 4 | **Prep Time: 20 min** | **Cook Time: 35 min**

Indian cuisine is thankfully more popular than ever before. Try this delicious Indian-inspired cauliflower and chickpea curry and I bet it will earn a spot in your weekly meal rotation.

3 tablespoons vegetable oil
1 onion, chopped
½ head cauliflower (1 lb/450 g), cut into florets
3 yellow-fleshed potatoes (about 15 oz/450 g), cut into cubes
1 (14 oz/398 mL) can coconut milk
1 (14 oz/398 mL) can chickpeas
1 cup (130 g) frozen peas
1 cup (250 mL) vegetable broth
3 tablespoons tomato paste
3 tablespoons nutritional yeast
2 tablespoons cane sugar or maple syrup
1 tablespoon minced ginger
2 cloves garlic, minced
1 teaspoon garam masala
1 teaspoon turmeric
1 teaspoon mustard seeds
1 teaspoon salt
¼ teaspoon red pepper flakes
Black pepper, to taste
Naan, for serving

1. In a saucepan over medium-high heat, heat the oil, then add the onions and sauté for 5 minutes.

2. Add the remaining ingredients and bring to a boil.

3. Lower the heat, cover, and keep cooking until the vegetables are tender, about 30 minutes.

4. Serve with naan.

Curried Tempeh

Serves 4 | **Prep Time: 20 min** | **Cook Time: 25 min**

If tempeh has never been for you, give it one last chance with this curried tempeh. I guarantee you won't regret it!

3 tablespoons vegetable oil
1 (8½ oz/240 g) package tempeh, diced
1 red bell pepper, sliced
1 zucchini, sliced into rounds
2 shallots, minced
2 cloves garlic, minced
1 tablespoon minced ginger
1 (14 oz/398 mL) can coconut milk
2 tablespoons brown sugar
1 tablespoon tomato paste
1 tablespoon curry powder
1 teaspoon salt
¼ teaspoon turmeric
¼ teaspoon red pepper flakes
Black pepper, to taste
1 Thai pepper, sliced, to garnish (optional)
Rice, for serving (optional)

1. In a skillet over high heat, heat the oil, then add the tempeh and the bell peppers and sauté for 7 minutes.

2. Add the zucchini, shallots, garlic, and ginger and keep cooking for 3 minutes.

3. Add the remaining ingredients, bring to a boil, lower the heat, and simmer for 15 minutes.

4. Serve with rice.

Korean-Inspired Pancakes

Serves 4 to 6 | **Prep Time: 30 min** | **Cook Time: 20 min**

Do you like your pancakes sweet or salty? With Korean pancakes, also known as *buchimgae*, you can enjoy a saltier take. Traditionally, *buchimgae* have egg, vegetable, meat, or fish fillings. With this recipe, I offer you three winning combinations: shiitake, cabbage, and corn, all served with a spicy red pepper sauce. Enjoying this dish is like traveling without ever leaving your kitchen!

Pancake Batter:
3 cups (375 g) all-purpose flour
3 cups (750 mL) plant milk
¼ cup (60 mL) vegetable oil
1 teaspoon baking powder
1 teaspoon salt

Shiitake Filling:
5 shiitake mushrooms, sliced

Green Onion and Cabbage Filling:
2 cups (130 g) minced Savoy cabbage
3 green onions, chopped
1 teaspoon salt

Green Onion and Corn Filling:
6 green onions, chopped
½ cup (80 g) frozen corn kernels, thawed

Vegetable oil, for sautéing fillings and frying
Spicy Red Pepper Sauce (page 66), for serving

For the Pancake Batter:

1. In a bowl, whisk together all the pancake batter ingredients.

For the Fillings:

2. In a skillet over high heat, heat the oil, then add the shiitake mushrooms and sauté for 5 minutes. Set aside.

3. Repeat with the green onion and cabbage filling, followed by the green onion and corn filling, adding more oil to the pan if needed. Set each aside.

To Assemble:

4. Preheat the oven to 200°F (95°C). Place in the oven a baking dish large enough to hold the pancakes.

5. In an oiled skillet over medium heat, drop a couple of spoonfuls of the filling of your choice. Pour ¼ to ½ cup (60 to 125 mL) pancake batter over the vegetables.

6. Cook for 3 minutes, then flip over the pancake. Keep cooking for 2 to 3 minutes or until the pancake is golden and cooked through. Place in the oven to keep warm until ready to serve.

7. Repeat, adding more oil to the pan as needed.

8. Serve with spicy red pepper sauce.

Spanakopita

Serves 6 | **Prep Time: 45 min** | **Cook Time: 45 min** | **Rest Time: 30 min**

This dish tastes like a vacation. Just imagine you are eating my version while in beautiful Greece!

Cashew Cream:
½ cup (70 g) cashews
1 cup (250 mL) plant milk
⅓ cup (20 g) nutritional yeast
2 tablespoons cornstarch
2 tablespoons maple syrup
1 teaspoon garlic powder
1 teaspoon onion powder

Filling:
¼ cup (60 mL) olive oil
2 onions, minced
1 pound (450 g) baby spinach
1 recipe Tofu Feta (page 157)
1 tablespoon chopped fresh dill
1 teaspoon dried oregano
Salt and black pepper, to taste

6 sheets phyllo pastry
Vegetable oil, for brushing

For the Cashew Cream:

1. Soak the cashews in boiling water for 5 minutes. Drain.

2. In a blender, combine the soaked cashews with the remaining ingredients and blend until creamy. Set aside.

For the Filling:

3. In a large skillet over medium-high heat, warm the olive oil, then add the onions and cook, stirring, for 5 minutes.

4. Add the spinach in batches, then add the tofu feta, dill, and oregano and keep cooking for 5 minutes.

5. Add the cashew cream, stir well, and keep cooking for 4 minutes.

6. Season with salt and pepper to taste. Transfer mixture to a bowl and chill in the fridge for 30 minutes.

To Assemble:

7. Preheat the oven to 350°F (180°C). Lightly oil a 9 × 13-inch (23 × 33 cm) baking dish.

8. Cut the phyllo sheets in half to fit the baking dish.

9. Layer 6 sheets in the bottom of the baking dish, brushing each sheet with oil before adding another.

10. Top with the filling, then layer the 6 remaining sheets over the filling, brushing each sheet with oil before adding the next.

11. Brush the top of the spanakopita with oil.

12. Bake for 30 minutes or until the top is golden brown.

Moussaka

Serves 4 | **Prep Time: 45 min** | **Cook Time: 1 hour, 45 min**

Moussaka is like a Greek shepherd's pie or *pâté chinois*, as they call it in Quebec. Instead of beef, corn, and potatoes, moussaka is made with lentils, eggplants, and potatoes. I brought this recipe back from Santorini, a Greek island where my wife and I attended a cooking class offered by a lovely couple. The delightful pair even went to the trouble of adapting their menu to suit our vegan diet. Here's their recipe, which I've tweaked to make even better!

Filling:

½ cup (125 mL) olive oil
1 large eggplant, skin on
3 yellow-fleshed potatoes (about 15 oz/450 g), skin on
Salt and black pepper, to taste

Tomato Sauce:

1 (12 oz/340 mL) jar roasted red bell peppers, drained
3 tablespoons olive oil
1 onion, chopped
¾ cup (180 mL) dry white wine
2 (19 oz/540 mL) cans green lentils, rinsed and drained
¼ cup (60 mL) tomato paste
2 tablespoons cane sugar
2 teaspoons dried oregano
2 bay leaves
1½ teaspoons salt
1 teaspoon ground cumin
½ teaspoon red pepper flakes

For the Filling:

1. Preheat the oven to 375°F (190°C). Grease 2 baking sheets with the oil. The eggplants will absorb all of the oil.

2. Cut the eggplant and potatoes lengthwise into ½-inch (1 cm) thick slices.

3. Set the eggplant and potato slices side by side on the prepared sheets. Generously season with salt and pepper.

4. Bake for 30 minutes. Set aside.

For the Tomato Sauce:

5. Use an immersion blender to puree the roasted red bell peppers. Set aside.

6. In a saucepan over medium heat, heat the oil, then add the onions and cook, stirring, until tender, about 5 minutes.

7. Add the white wine and keep cooking for 3 minutes.

8. Add the remaining ingredients and simmer over medium heat for 20 minutes. Discard the bay leaves. Set aside.

Recipe continues

Recipe continued

"Béchamel" Sauce:
½ cup (60 g) cashews
2 cups (500 mL) plant milk
⅓ cup (20 g) nutritional yeast
2 tablespoons cornstarch
1 tablespoon cane sugar
1 teaspoon garlic powder
1 teaspoon salt
¼ teaspoon ground nutmeg

Smoked paprika, to garnish

For the "Béchamel" Sauce:

9. Soak the cashews in boiling water for 5 minutes. Drain.

10. In a blender, combine the soaked cashews with the milk, nutritional yeast, cornstarch, sugar, garlic powder, salt, and nutmeg and blend until creamy.

11. Transfer the mixture to a saucepan. Set over medium heat and bring to a boil while whisking constantly.

12. Once the sauce boils, keep cooking and whisking for about 2 minutes or until the mixture thickens.

To Assemble:

13. In an 8 × 12-inch (20 × 30 cm) baking dish, place the toasted potato slices.

14. Pour the tomato sauce over the potatoes.

15. Cover with the eggplant, without overlapping them.

16. Spread the béchamel sauce over top.

17. Sprinkle with smoked paprika. Bake for 45 minutes.

"Chick'un" Roast with Mushroom Sauce

Serves 4 | **Prep Time: 40 min** | **Cook Time: 1 hour, 25 min** | **Rest Time: 15 min**

When I was little, I had a passion for the Smurfs and their Mushroom Village. Hey, maybe that's where my love of mushrooms comes from! I also loved LEGO bricks, but I can't say I've ever eaten plastic, so maybe that theory doesn't actually hold water. If you also love mushrooms, I promise you'll simply adore this recipe.

"Chick'un" Roast:

1¼ cups (160 g) gluten flour
¼ cup (15 g) nutritional yeast
1 tablespoon onion powder
1 tablespoon garlic powder
1 teaspoon salt
½ teaspoon poultry seasoning
1 (7 oz/200 g) block firm tofu
¾ cup (180 mL) plant milk
1 tablespoon miso paste
6 cups (1.5 L) vegetable broth
2 tablespoons soy sauce
2 tablespoons vegetable oil
1 tablespoon maple syrup
1 teaspoon mustard seeds
1 teaspoon herbes de provence

For the "Chick'un" Roast:

1. In a large bowl, combine the gluten flour, nutritional yeast, onion powder, garlic powder, salt, and poultry seasoning. Set aside.

2. Coarsely crumble the tofu and transfer to a blender. Add the milk and miso paste and blend to a smooth consistency.

3. Add the tofu mixture to the dry ingredients and stir well to combine.

4. Transfer the dough to a clean work surface and knead for 2 minutes. Wrap the dough in plastic wrap or cheesecloth, then gather up the corners and tie to close.

5. In a saucepan, bring the vegetable broth to a boil, then add the wrapped tofu roast. Lower the heat and simmer the tofu roast for 1 hour, flipping it from time to time. The tofu roast must remain covered with broth throughout. Add more broth if needed. You can also steam it by wrapping the tofu in plastic or cheesecloth and placing it in a steamer basket for 1 hour. Remove from the heat and let the tofu roast cool in the broth for 15 minutes.

6. Unwrap the tofu roast and discard the plastic wrap or cheesecloth.

7. Before serving, in a skillet, whisk together the soy sauce, oil, maple syrup, mustard seeds, and herbes de provence. Add the tofu roast. Coat with glaze and roast over medium-high heat for 5 minutes.

Recipe continues

Recipe continued

Mushroom Sauce:

1 teaspoon cornstarch
2 tablespoons water
3 tablespoons vegetable oil
**4 cups (225 g) chopped
 mushrooms**
2 shallots, minced
½ cup (125 mL) white wine
1 cup (250 mL) vegetable broth
2 tablespoons nutritional yeast
2 tablespoons miso paste
2 tablespoons tomato paste
2 tablespoons soy sauce
**2 tablespoons vegan
 Worcestershire sauce**
2 cloves garlic, minced
Salt and black pepper, to taste

Sprigs of thyme, to garnish

For the Mushroom Sauce:

8. In a small bowl, combine the cornstarch with the water. Set aside.

9. In a saucepan over medium heat, heat the oil, then add the mushrooms and shallots and cook, stirring, for 3 minutes. Add the white wine and reduce for 2 minutes. Add the remaining ingredients, except the cornstarch mixture and thyme. Stir to combine, bring to a boil, then simmer for 12 minutes.

10. Whisk the cornstarch mixture into the sauce. Bring to a boil. Set aside.

To Serve:

11. Slice the tofu roast and serve with the mushroom sauce.

12. Garnish with sprigs of thyme.

Calzones

Serves 2 (calzones), makes 2¼ cups (225 g) vegan mozzarella | Prep Time: 1 hour | Cook Time: 1 hour, 10 min | Rest Time: 2 hours, 35 min

A calzone is kind of like a fancy pizza . . . well a pizza that is folded in half! A calzone is as suitable for your guests as it is for a solitary nighttime snack.

Vegan Mozzarella:
¼ cup (30 g) cashews
1 teaspoon lemon juice
1 teaspoon maple syrup
⅓ cup (80 mL) vegetable oil
1½ cups (375 mL) water
2 tablespoons nutritional yeast
1 tablespoon powdered
    agar-agar
2 tablespoons tapioca starch
1 teaspoon salt

Pizza Dough:
1¾ cups (430 mL) warm water
1 tablespoon granulated sugar
1 (¼ oz/8 g) packet active dry
    yeast
3 cups (375 g) all-purpose flour
1 teaspoon salt

For the Vegan Mozzarella:

1. Soak the cashews in boiling water for 10 minutes. Drain.

2. In a blender, combine the cashews with the remaining ingredients and blend until creamy.

3. Pour the mixture in a saucepan and bring to a boil, stirring constantly. When it is starting to bubble, keep cooking for 1 to 2 minutes more, stirring constantly. The mixture will be thicker at this point.

4. Divide the mixture between 2 ramekins and refrigerate for at least 2 hours or a maximum of 5 days.

For the Pizza Dough:

5. In a bowl, combine the warm water, sugar, and yeast. Let rest until the mixture foams, about 5 minutes.

6. In a large bowl, combine the flour with the salt. Add the yeast mixture to the flour and mix to combine.

7. Cover the bowl with a clean, damp cloth. Let the dough rise for 30 minutes in a warm, draft-free spot.

8. Transfer the dough to a lightly floured work surface or to the bowl of a stand mixer. Knead until the dough becomes smooth, about 5 minutes. Sprinkle with more flour, if needed, to prevent the dough from sticking. Set aside.

Recipe continues

Recipe continued

Tomato Sauce:

3 tablespoons olive oil

1 yellow onion, chopped

2 cloves garlic, minced

1 (28 oz/796 mL) can diced tomatoes

1 tablespoon cane sugar

2 bay leaves

1 teaspoon dried basil

1 teaspoon dried oregano

¼ teaspoon red pepper flakes

Filling:

3 tablespoons vegetable oil

4 cups (225 g) chopped mushrooms

1 zucchini, sliced

½ red bell pepper, chopped

½ green bell pepper, chopped

½ red onion, chopped

2 cloves garlic, minced

1 teaspoon dried oregano

1 teaspoon salt

For the Tomato Sauce:

9. In a saucepan over medium heat, heat the oil, then add the onions and cook until translucent, about 6 minutes.

10. Add the garlic and keep cooking for 2 minutes.

11. Add the remaining ingredients. Bring to a boil, lower the heat, and simmer for 30 minutes.

For the Filling:

12. In a skillet over high heat, heat the oil, then add the mushrooms and sauté for 5 minutes.

13. Add the oregano and salt and keep cooking for 3 minutes. Set aside.

To Assemble:

14. Preheat the oven to 375°F (190°C). Flour a baking sheet.

15. Divide the dough into 2 equal portions. Roll out each portion of dough into an 11-inch (28 cm) circle.

16. Slather half of the sauce over each circle.

17. Top each with half of the vegetable filling.

18. Top with vegan mozzarella and fold each circle in half.

19. Transfer the calzones to the prepared sheet and bake for 15 to 20 minutes, until the tops are golden.

Spaghetti with "Meatballs"

Serves 4 | **Prep Time: 45 min** | **Cook Time: 1 hour, 25 min**

I used to think that nothing could ever surpass the spaghetti I had as a child . . . until now.

"Meatballs":
¼ cup (60 mL) olive oil
1 onion, chopped
3 carrots, grated
1 zucchini, grated
1 (19 oz/540 mL) can green
    lentils, rinsed and drained
¼ cup (15 g) nutritional yeast
3 tablespoons tomato paste
2 cloves garlic, minced
1 teaspoon salt
½ teaspoon red pepper flakes
¾ cup (100 g) gluten flour

Sauce:
¼ cup (60 mL) olive oil
1 onion, chopped
2 (28 oz/796 mL) cans diced
    tomatoes
2 tablespoons tomato paste
2 tablespoons cane sugar
4 cloves garlic, minced
2 teaspoons salt
2 teaspoons dried basil
¼ teaspoon red pepper flakes

1 (1 lb/450 g) package dry
    spaghetti pasta
Cashew Parmesan (page 155),
    to garnish
Fresh basil leaves, to garnish

For the "Meatballs":

1. Preheat the oven to 350°F (180°C). Grease a baking sheet with oil.

2. In a skillet over medium-high heat, heat the oil, then add the onions and cook, stirring, for 5 minutes. Add the grated carrots and zucchini and keep cooking for 5 minutes.

3. Add the lentils, nutritional yeast, tomato paste, garlic, salt, and red pepper flakes, stir to combine, and remove from the heat.

4. Transfer the mixture to a food processor. Add the gluten flour and blend for 1 to 2 minutes until combined.

5. Use an ice-cream scoop to shape 15 meatballs, placing them evenly on the prepared sheet.

6. Bake for 30 minutes. Set aside.

For the Sauce:

7. In a saucepan over medium heat, heat the oil, then add the onions and cook, stirring, for 5 minutes.

8. Add the remaining ingredients and stir to combine. Bring to a boil, lower the heat, and simmer for 30 minutes.

9. Add the meatballs to the sauce. Keep cooking for 10 minutes. Set aside.

To Serve:

10. Cook the pasta according to the package directions. Drain.

11. Divide the pasta among the serving bowls. Pour sauce over each and distribute the meatballs. Sprinkle each serving with cashew parmesan.

Tempeh Spaghetti

Serves 6 (pasta), makes ¾ cup (90 g) cashew parmesan | Prep Time: 30 min | Cook Time: 55 min

Everyone loved my grandmother's spaghetti sauce. Her secret? A pinch of sugar! This recipe also features cashew parmesan, which isn't like dairy parmesan . . . it's better!

Sauce:

- 1 (8½ oz/240 g) package tempeh
- 1 (17 oz/500 mL) jar roasted red bell peppers, drained
- ¼ cup (60 mL) olive oil
- 8 cups (450 g) sliced mushrooms
- 2 onions, minced
- 4 (28 oz/796 mL) cans diced tomatoes
- 2 cups (220 g) grated carrots
- 1 (5½ oz/156 mL) can tomato paste
- ⅓ cup (65 g) cane sugar
- 5 cloves garlic, minced
- 1 tablespoon harissa sauce
- 1 tablespoon dried basil
- 1 tablespoon dried oregano
- 1½ teaspoons salt
- 1 teaspoon ground cumin
- ¼ teaspoon ground cloves

Cashew Parmesan:

- ⅓ cup (40 g) cashews
- ⅓ cup (20 g) nutritional yeast
- 1 clove garlic, minced
- ½ teaspoon salt

- 1 (1 lb/450 g) package dry spaghetti pasta
- Fresh basil leaves, to garnish

For the Sauce:

1. Coarsely chop the tempeh, then crumble it using your hands. Set aside.

2. Use an immersion blender to puree the roasted red bell peppers. Set aside.

3. In a large pot over medium-high heat, heat the oil, then add the crumbled tempeh, mushrooms, and onions and cook, stirring, for 10 minutes.

4. Add the pureed roasted red bell peppers along with the remaining ingredients. Stir to combine. Bring to a boil, lower the heat, and cook for 45 minutes, stirring regularly. Set aside.

For the Cashew Parmesan:

5. Pulse all the ingredients in a food processor until you reach a coarse but uniform consistency.

6. Set aside in the fridge until ready to use. It will keep in an airtight container in the fridge for up to 2 weeks.

To Serve:

7. Cook the pasta according to the package directions. Drain.

8. Serve the sauce over the cooked pasta. Sprinkle with cashew parmesan.

Pesto Pasta

Serves 4 | Prep Time: 15 min | Cook Time: 15 min | Rest Time: 2 hours

Why eat humble spaghetti when you can instead make pesto pasta? Much more elegant!

Tofu Feta:
1 (1 lb/450 g) block firm tofu
4 cloves garlic, minced
3 tablespoons apple cider vinegar
2 tablespoons olive oil
4 teaspoons salt
2 teaspoons dried oregano
2 teaspoons maple syrup

Pesto:
½ cup (30 g) fresh basil leaves
½ cup (60 g) cashews
½ cup (125 mL) olive oil
¼ cup (15 g) nutritional yeast
1 clove garlic, minced
Pinch of salt
Black pepper, to taste

1 (1 lb/450 g) package dry penne pasta or other pasta of your choice
Fresh basil leaves, to garnish

For the Tofu Feta:

1. Cut the tofu into cubes.

2. Add the tofu and the remaining ingredients to a jar, cover with water, then close the lid. Gently shake the jar to distribute the seasonings. Marinate in the fridge for at least 2 hours and up to 2 days.

For the Pesto:

3. In a food processor, place all the ingredients and blend until smooth. Set aside.

To Serve:

4. Cook the pasta according to the package directions. Drain and set aside.

5. In a saucepan over medium-high heat, add the pesto and stir for 2 minutes to warm it up. Add the cooked pasta. Stir to coat and reheat the pasta, adding a bit of water if the sauce isn't coating the pasta.

6. Divide the pasta among serving bowls. Crumble the tofu feta and sprinkle it over top, then garnish with basil.

Bolognese Rigatoni

Serves 4 | **Prep Time: 25 min** | **Cook Time: 30 min**

This delicious dish is solid proof that lentils are not just a good source of protein and fiber but also a good source of comfort!

Bolognese Sauce:

3 tablespoons olive oil

1 onion, minced

1 (19 oz/540 mL) can green lentils, rinsed and drained

1 (11½ oz/340 mL) jar roasted red bell peppers

1 cup (250 mL) dry white wine

¾ cup (180 mL) soy cream

½ cup (125 mL) tomato paste

2 tablespoons cane sugar

3 cloves garlic, minced

2 bay leaves

1 teaspoon dried oregano

1 teaspoon dried basil

1 teaspoon salt

½ teaspoon red pepper flakes

½ teaspoon ground cumin

Black pepper, to taste

1 (1 lb/450 g) package dry rigatoni pasta, for serving

Chopped fresh parsley, to garnish

1. In a saucepan over medium-high heat, heat the oil, then add the onions and cook, stirring, for 5 minutes.

2. Use an immersion blender to puree the roasted red bell peppers.

3. Add the pureed red pepper, along with the remaining ingredients, and bring to a boil. Lower the heat and simmer for 15 minutes, stirring from time to time.

4. Cook the pasta according to the package directions. Drain.

5. Add the pasta to the Bolognese sauce, stir, and serve, sprinkled with the chopped parsley.

Vegan "Seafood" Linguine

Serves 2 | Prep Time: 20 min | Cook Time: 20 min

My father is from Gaspé Peninsula, a beautiful region along the coast of the Gulf of St. Lawrence in Quebec. We used to vacation there each summer, and it was during one of those visits that I first tasted seafood spaghetti. I remember it to this day, and I have long tried to recreate the same flavors in a vegan version of the dish. Lucky for you, I believe I have finally succeeded! The secret: white wine, which coincidentally makes for a successful trip to Gaspé—along with a great deal of mosquito repellent!

Béchamel Sauce:
- 3 tablespoons olive oil
- ¼ cup (32 g) all-purpose flour
- 2 cups (500 mL) vegetable broth
- ¼ cup (15 g) nutritional yeast
- 2 tablespoons maple syrup
- 1 teaspoon salt
- ¼ teaspoon truffle oil (optional)

Vegetable "Seafood":
- 5 king oyster mushrooms
- 3 tablespoons olive oil
- 2 shallots, minced
- ¾ cup (180 mL) dry white wine
- 1 tablespoon maple syrup
- ½ sheet nori, torn into small pieces
- 2 cloves garlic, minced

- 1 (1 lb/450 g) package dry linguine pasta
- Chopped fresh parsley, to garnish

For the Béchamel Sauce:
1. In a saucepan, whisk the oil and flour together. Cook over medium heat for 3 minutes, whisking constantly.

2. Whisk in the vegetable broth and keep cooking, whisking constantly. Add the nutritional yeast, maple syrup, salt, and truffle oil (if using).

3. Keep cooking over low heat for 4 minutes, stirring frequently. Set aside.

For the Vegetable "Seafood":
4. Slice the mushrooms into thick rounds to make them look like scallops.

5. In a saucepan over high heat, heat the oil, then add the mushrooms and sauté for 5 minutes to give them color. Lower the heat to medium, then add the shallots and keep cooking for 5 minutes.

6. Add the wine, maple syrup, nori, and garlic. Keep cooking for 4 minutes. Stir in the béchamel sauce and bring the mixture to a boil. Meanwhile, make the pasta.

To Serve:
7. Cook the pasta according to the package directions. Drain.

8. Right before serving, pour the sauce over the cooked pasta and sprinkle with parsley.

Sweet Potato and Mushroom Stuffed Shells

Serves 4 | **Prep Time: 40 min** | **Cook Time: 1 hour** | **Rest Time: 20 min**

I discovered this dish at a restaurant in New York. (Yes, I love to travel . . . and brag about it!) When I returned home, I knew I needed to create my own version of this unique dish. Give it a try: it'll turn you into a world-class cook in the comfort of your own home.

12 jumbo pasta shells

3 tablespoons vegetable oil

1 onion, chopped

4 cups (225 g) chopped mushrooms

2 sweet potatoes (1 oz/500 g), peeled and cut into small cubes

1 cup (120 g) cashews, coarsely chopped

8 cups (140 g) baby spinach

1 cup (250 mL) vegetable broth

3 cloves garlic, minced

1 tablespoon maple syrup

⅓ cup (20 g) nutritional yeast

1½ teaspoons salt, or more to taste

¼ teaspoon truffle oil (optional)

Black pepper, to taste

3 cups (750 mL) Tomato Sauce (page 150)

Cashew Parmesan (page 155), for serving

1. Cook the pasta shells according to the package directions. Drain and set aside.

2. In a saucepan over medium heat, heat the oil, then add the onions and cook, stirring, for 5 minutes.

3. Add the mushrooms, sweet potatoes, and cashews and keep cooking for 10 minutes, stirring constantly.

4. Add the spinach, vegetable broth, garlic, and maple syrup and keep cooking over medium-high heat, stirring constantly, until the liquid is fully absorbed and the sweet potato cubes are tender, about 15 minutes. Add more vegetable broth if needed. Remove from the heat.

5. Add the nutritional yeast, salt, truffle oil (if using), and pepper. Stir to combine. Refrigerate the filling for 20 minutes.

6. Preheat the oven to 375°F (190°C).

7. Use a ¼-cup (60 mL) measuring cup to fill each pasta shell with the vegetable filling.

8. Spread half of the sauce over the bottom of a baking dish. Set the shells side by side on the sauce, then spoon the remaining sauce over.

9. Bake for 30 minutes.

10. Sprinkle with cashew parmesan and serve.

Sun-Dried Tomato Risotto

Serves 4 | Prep Time: 20 min | Cook Time: 30 min

Red is my favorite color. When I was a child, I often wore red overalls. Fortunately, times change, and the overalls have long been retired. To make this delicious, red risotto experience complete, serve it with a Bloody Mary.

Sun-Dried Tomato Pesto:
½ cup (45 g) chopped sun-dried tomatoes
10 fresh basil leaves
2 tablespoons nutritional yeast
2 cloves garlic, minced
¼ cup (60 mL) olive oil
¼ cup (30 g) chopped cashews
1 teaspoon maple syrup
Black pepper, to taste

Risotto:
3 cups (750 mL) vegetable broth
2 tablespoons olive oil
1 onion, chopped
1½ cups (280 g) arborio rice
½ cup (125 mL) dry white wine
Salt, to taste

Fresh basil leaves, to garnish

For the Sun-Dried Tomato Pesto:
1. In a food processor or blender, blend all the pesto ingredients until smooth. Set aside.

For the Risotto:
2. In a saucepan, warm the vegetable broth. Set aside.

3. In a large saucepan over medium heat, heat the oil, then add the onions and cook, stirring, for 5 minutes. Add the rice and cook, stirring, for 2 minutes.

4. Add the white wine, scrape the bottom of the pot to deglaze, then reduce for 2 minutes. Add the warm broth, 1 cup (250 mL) at a time, stirring regularly and waiting until the broth is fully absorbed before adding more. Repeat these steps until all the broth is used. After about 20 minutes, the rice should be al dente and the risotto should be creamy.

To Serve:
5. In a skillet, stir the sun-dried tomato pesto for 2 minutes to warm it up. Adjust the seasoning if needed.

6. Stir the pesto into the risotto. Serve immediately with basil.

One-Pot Lasagna

Serves 4 | **Prep Time: 15 min** | **Cook Time: 30 min**

Lasagna is so irresistible. It also used to be quite a chore to prepare, but not anymore. Put all the ingredients in a pan and voilà! Thirty minutes later, dinner is served!

3 tablespoons olive oil

1 (8½ oz/240 g) package tempeh, diced

1 green bell pepper, diced

1 onion, minced

2 tablespoons cane sugar

1 tablespoon dried oregano

1 tablespoon dried basil

2 cloves garlic, minced

¼ teaspoon red pepper flakes

2 cups (500 mL) store-bought strained tomatoes

2 cups (500 mL) vegetable broth

5½ oz (150 g) dry lasagna sheets, snapped into pieces

Salt and black pepper, to taste

Chopped fresh parsley, to garnish

1. In a saucepan over medium-high heat, heat the oil, then add the tempeh, bell peppers, and onions and cook, stirring, for 5 minutes.

2. Add the sugar, oregano, basil, garlic, and red pepper flakes and stir to combine. Stir in the tomato sauce and vegetable broth.

3. Add the pasta, bring to a boil, lower the heat, cover, and simmer for 20 minutes. Season to taste, sprinkle with the parsley, and serve.

"Meat" Pie

Serves 4 to 6 | **Prep Time: 40 min** | **Cook Time: 1 hour, 10 min** | **Rest Time: 1 hour**

Meat pie, sea-pie, or *cipaille*, as they call it in Quebec, is a traditional layered meat or fish pie. Would I dare alter this classic to create a vegan version? You bet I would! And if you ask me, it's even better than the original.

Filling

3 tablespoons vegetable oil

2 onions, minced

2½ cups (625 mL) vegetable broth

1¼ cups (100 g) textured vegetable protein (TVP) cut into small cubes

4 yellow-fleshed potatoes (about 20 oz/600 g), peeled and cut into cubes

¼ cup (15 g) nutritional yeast

1 tablespoon maple syrup

2 cloves garlic, minced

2 bay leaves

2 teaspoons salt

1 teaspoon dried basil

1 teaspoon dried oregano

1 teaspoon poultry seasoning

½ teaspoon dry mustard

Black pepper, to taste

½ recipe Pie Pastry (page 175)

1. In a saucepan over medium heat, heat the oil, then add the onions and cook, stirring, for 5 minutes.

2. Add the remaining ingredients and bring to a boil. Keep cooking for 10 minutes.

3. Refrigerate the mixture for at least 1 hour to set.

4. Preheat the oven to 350°F (180°C).

5. Meanwhile, roll out 1 pie crust until it is 9 × 9 inches (23 × 23 cm) and ½ inch (1 cm) thick.

6. Transfer the mixture to the baking dish and cover with the pie crust. Use a fork to crimp the edges.

7. Bake for 50 to 60 minutes, until golden.

Samosa Pie

Makes 1 (9-inch/23 cm) pie | **Prep Time: 45 min** | **Cook Time: 1 hour, 15 min**

Samosas are little stuffed pastries. And what's better than a little pastry? How about a big one! This recipe is my Québécois version of this Indian culinary classic.

2 yellow-fleshed potatoes (about 10½ oz/300 g), peeled and diced

2 carrots, diced

3 tablespoons vegetable oil

2 cups (115 g) chopped mushrooms

1 onion, minced

1 (19 oz/540 mL) can chickpeas, rinsed and drained

1 (14 oz/398 mL) can coconut milk

½ head cauliflower (1 lb/450 g), cut into florets

1 cup (130 g) frozen peas

¼ cup (15 g) nutritional yeast

3 tablespoons tomato paste

3 tablespoons maple syrup

3 cloves garlic, minced

1 tablespoon minced ginger

2 teaspoons salt

1 teaspoon curry powder

1 teaspoon mustard seeds

½ teaspoon turmeric

½ teaspoon red pepper flakes

Black pepper, to taste

1 recipe Pie Pastry (page 175)

1. Preheat the oven to 375°F (190°C).

2. Place the potatoes and carrots in a saucepan. Cover with water.

3. Bring to a boil. Lower the heat, then simmer for 15 minutes or until the vegetables are partially cooked. Drain and set aside.

4. In a skillet over medium-high heat, heat the oil, then add the mushrooms and onions and cook, stirring, for 5 minutes. Add the chickpeas, coconut milk, cauliflower, peas, nutritional yeast, tomato paste, maple syrup, garlic, ginger, and spices. Stir to combine. Add the cooked carrots and potatoes.

5. Roll out the pie pastry into two ¼-inch (6 mm) thick circles.

6. Line a 9-inch (23 cm) pie plate with 1 circle of dough. Fill with the vegetable mixture. Cover with the second circle of dough. Using a sharp knife, cut air vents in the center of the top crust. Seal the top and bottom crusts together by pressing a fork all around the edge of the pie, or use your fingers to crimp it.

7. Bake for 50 minutes to 1 hour or until the crust is golden brown.

Pâté Chinois

Serves 6 | **Prep Time: 45 min** | **Cook Time: 90 min**

This book would not have been complete without this recipe, THE classic of Quebec cuisine: *pâté chinois* (this name has always left me puzzled). It's similar to the English classic shepherd's pie, but instead of lamb it is made with ground beef and corn. My babysitter's version was good, and my mom's was delicious, but my grandmother's was outstanding—all served with ketchup, of course. Inspired by all the *pâtés chinois* I enjoyed when I was young, I've created the ultimate vegan version—try it yourself and let me know what you think!

Filling:

¼ cup (60 mL) vegetable oil

8 cups (450 g) chopped
    mushrooms

3 stalks celery, chopped

2 onions, chopped

1½ teaspoons salt

8 cups (140 g) baby spinach

1 (19 oz/540 mL) can green
    lentils, rinsed and drained

1 cup (120 g) cashews, coarsely
    chopped

½ cup (125 mL) vegetable broth

⅓ cup (20 g) nutritional yeast

2 tablespoons maple syrup

2 cloves garlic, minced

1 teaspoon dried basil

1 teaspoon dried oregano

½ teaspoon tourtière spice mix
    or ¼ teaspoon ground cloves

½ teaspoon truffle oil (optional)

Black pepper, to taste

For the Filling:

1. In a saucepan over medium-high heat, heat the oil, then add the mushrooms, celery, onions, and salt and cook, stirring, for 10 minutes.

2. Add the remaining ingredients and keep cooking, stirring constantly, for 10 minutes. Set aside.

Recipe continues

Recipe continued

Potato Puree:

7 yellow-fleshed potatoes (about 2½ lb/1 kg), skin on

½ cup (125 mL) soy cream

¼ cup (60 mL) vegan butter

¼ cup (15 g) nutritional yeast

2 teaspoons salt

1 teaspoon onion powder

To Assemble:

2 cups (330 g) frozen corn kernels, thawed

1 (14 oz/398 mL) can creamed corn

Smoked paprika, to taste

For the Potato Puree:

3. Place the potatoes in a saucepan, then cover with cold water.

4. Bring to a boil and cook until the potatoes are tender, 30 to 45 minutes.

5. Drain and let cool for a few minutes. When the potatoes are cool to the touch, use your hands to peel the skins.

6. Transfer the peeled potatoes to a bowl, add the remaining ingredients, and use a potato masher to mash the potatoes to a smooth consistency.

To Assemble:

7. Preheat the oven to 375°F (190°C).

8. Lightly press the filling over the bottom of an 8-inch (20 cm) square baking dish. Cover with the corn kernels, then with the creamed corn. Spread the potato puree over the corn. Sprinkle with smoked paprika.

9. Bake for 40 minutes. Let cool for 10 minutes before serving.

Tofu Pot Pie

Makes 1 (10¼-inch/26 cm) pie | **Prep Time: 45 min** |
Cook Time: 1 hour, 10 min | **Rest Time: 1 hour**

Having trouble getting your kids to eat tofu? Sneak it into this pie—they'll love it.

Pie Pastry:

7 tablespoons (105 mL) ice water
1 tablespoon white vinegar
3 cups (375 g) all-purpose flour
1 teaspoon salt
1 cup (250 mL) vegan butter

Béchamel Sauce:

3 tablespoons vegetable oil
¼ cup (32 g) all-purpose flour
2 cups (500 mL) vegetable broth
¼ cup (15 g) nutritional yeast
1 teaspoon salt
Black pepper, to taste

For the Pie Pastry:

1. Combine the water and vinegar. Set aside.

2. In a large bowl, combine the flour with the salt. Using a pastry cutter or 2 knives, incorporate the vegan butter into the flour until the mixture is crumbly, with pea-size chunks throughout.

3. Stir in the water and vinegar mixture.

4. Bring the pastry together into a ball, being careful not to overwork the pastry. If the pastry seems dry, add a few drops of water. Cover with plastic wrap. Refrigerate the pastry for at least 30 minutes and no longer than 1 hour.

For the Béchamel Sauce:

5. In a small saucepan over medium heat, heat the oil, then add the flour and whisk for 1 minute.

6. Whisk in the vegetable broth and keep cooking, whisking constantly, until the sauce thickens.

7. Bring to a boil, lower the heat, stir in the nutritional yeast, and keep cooking for 3 minutes.

8. Season with salt and pepper. Let cool in the fridge for 30 minutes.

Recipe continues

Recipe continued

Filling:

**2 yellow-fleshed potatoes
(about 10½ oz/300 g),
peeled and diced**

2 carrots, diced

3 tablespoons vegetable oil

**4 cups (225 g) sliced
mushrooms**

1 onion, chopped

½ cup (125 mL) white wine

**1 (12½ oz/350 g) block firm
tofu, cut into cubes**

1 cup (130 g) frozen peas

1 tablespoon maple syrup

1 teaspoon poultry seasoning

Salt, to taste

For the Filling:

9. Place the potatoes and carrots in a saucepan. Cover with water. Bring to a boil, lower the heat, and simmer for 12 minutes. Drain and set aside.

10. In a saucepan over medium-high heat, heat the oil, then add the mushrooms and onions and cook, stirring, for 5 minutes. Add the white wine and simmer until the liquid is almost completely evaporated.

11. Add the remaining ingredients along with the potatoes, carrots, and béchamel sauce. Stir to combine. Bring to a boil, then lower the heat to medium and cook for 4 minutes.

12. Adjust seasoning if needed. Refrigerate the filling for at least 30 minutes.

To Assemble:

13. Preheat the oven to 375°F (190°C).

14. Roll out the pie pastry into two ¼-inch (6 mm) thick circles.

15. Line a 10¼-inch (26 cm) pie plate with 1 circle of dough. Fill with the cooled filling and cover with the second circle of dough.

16. Using a sharp knife, cut air vents in the center of the top crust. Seal the top and bottom crusts together by pressing a fork all around the edge of the pie, or use your fingers to crimp it.

17. Bake for 40 minutes, until the top is golden.

DESSERTS

Coconut Cookies

Makes 12 cookies | **Prep Time: 20 min** | **Cook Time: 12 min** | **Rest Time: 30 min**

When I was little, my grandmother would always offer me a cookie from her house-shaped cookie tin when I visited. Those were the best cookies in the world. Times change, but nothing beats these cookies and a good tin.

½ cup (125 mL) coconut oil

½ cup (110 g) packed brown sugar

¼ cup (50 g) granulated sugar

½ teaspoon vanilla extract

1¼ cups (160 g) all-purpose flour

½ teaspoon baking soda

½ teaspoon salt

1⅓ cups (120 g) unsweetened shredded coconut

⅔ cup (160 mL) canned coconut milk or plant milk

1. Preheat the oven to 375°F (190°C). Line a baking sheet with parchment paper.

2. In a bowl, beat the coconut oil, brown sugar, granulated sugar, and vanilla extract together for 3 minutes.

3. In a second bowl, whisk together the flour, baking soda, and salt.

4. Add the dry ingredients to the coconut oil mixture and stir to combine. Add the shredded coconut and coconut milk and mix well. Refrigerate for 30 minutes to set.

5. Shape the mixture into small balls. Set the balls on the prepared baking, leaving a bit of space between each.

6. Bake for 10 to 12 minutes or until lightly golden. Transfer the cookies to a wire rack and let cool for a few minutes. Enjoy.

Brownies

Makes 9 brownies | **Prep Time: 20 min** | **Cook Time: 30 min** | **Rest Time: 20 min**

There are two kinds of people: those who have a sweet tooth and those who have salty cravings. Actually, there's a third kind of person, and I count myself among them: those who could survive on brownies alone. Brownies are, beyond a shadow of a doubt, one of my favorites. They also have a special place in my heart because they are the first dessert I learned how to make.

⅓ cup (160 mL) coconut oil
3½ oz (100 g) chopped dark chocolate
½ cup (125 mL) plant milk
⅓ cup (80 mL) applesauce
1 teaspoon vanilla extract
1 cup (125 g) all-purpose flour
1 cup (200 g) granulated sugar
½ cup (110 g) packed brown sugar
½ cup (75 g) chopped walnuts
¼ cup (20 g) cocoa powder
1 teaspoon baking soda
1 teaspoon salt

1. Preheat the oven to 375°F (190°C). Line an 8-inch (20 cm) square baking pan with parchment paper.

2. Melt the coconut oil in the microwave or in a saucepan on the stovetop. Remove from the heat, add the chocolate, and let rest until the chocolate is melted. Return the mixture to the microwave or to the stovetop for a few seconds if necessary.

3. Transfer the chocolate mixture to a bowl. Whisk in the milk, applesauce, and vanilla extract. Set aside.

4. In a second bowl, stir together the flour, granulated sugar, brown sugar, walnuts, cocoa powder, baking soda, and salt.

5. Add the liquid ingredients to the dry ingredients. Beat for 1 minute.

6. Pour the brownie batter into the prepared pan. Bake for 30 minutes.

7. Let cool for 15 to 20 minutes. Unmold, cut into squares, and serve.

Donuts

Makes 20 donuts | **Prep Time: 40 min** | **Cook Time: 30 min** | **Rest Time: 2 hours**

Since muffins have as many calories as donuts, why not just eat donuts instead? Prepackaged donuts are never going to be as good as homemade ones! So why not bake them yourself—and with a vegan twist?

Donuts:

2 cups (500 mL) plant milk
2 (¼ oz/8 g) packets active dry yeast
1½ cups (300 g) granulated sugar
½ cup (125 mL) vegan butter, melted
2 teaspoons vanilla extract
2 teaspoons salt
7 cups (875 g) all-purpose flour
Vegetable oil, for frying

For the Donuts:

1. Warm the milk in the microwave for 30 seconds to 1 minute, or on the stovetop over medium heat.

2. Add the yeast to the warm milk, stir to combine, and let rest until the mixture foams, about 10 minutes.

3. Transfer the yeast mixture to a bowl, then add the sugar, melted vegan butter, vanilla extract, and salt and mix well to combine.

4. Add the flour and stir until a sticky ball forms.

5. Cover the bowl with a damp cloth and let rest at room temperature for about 2 hours, or until it doubles in size.

6. Transfer the dough to a lightly floured work surface and roll out to a ¼-inch (0.5 cm) thickness.

7. Cut out the donuts using a donut cutter or round cookie cutter.

8. To fry, in a large heavy-bottomed pot, add enough oil to cover the donuts. Preheat the oil to 350°F (180°C). In batches, being careful not to overcrowd the pot, use tongs to submerge the donuts in the oil, and fry until golden brown, about 2 to 3 minutes, flipping them halfway through.

9. Transfer the fried donuts to a rack and let cool before glazing.

Recipe continues

Recipe continued

Glaze:

3 cups (360 g) powdered sugar

5 tablespoons (75 mL) water

3 colors of food coloring of your choice

Sprinkles, for decoration (optional)

For the Glaze:

10. In a bowl, combine the powdered sugar and water.

11. Divide the glaze among 3 bowls.

12. Add a few drops of the first food coloring, depending how dark you want it, to a bowl and mix until combined. Repeat with the other 2 colors so you have 3 different colors.

To Assemble:

13. To glaze, dip half of the donut into the desired color and return to the wire rack to set. Add sprinkles if desired. Repeat.

14. Let the donuts set before diving in.

Macaroons

Makes 12 macaroons | **Prep Time: 10 min** | **Cook Time: 12 min** | **Rest Time: 45 min**

Here's a quick and easy recipe when you want to indulge your sweet tooth!

1 cup (200 g) cane sugar

½ cup (125 mL) melted coconut oil

⅓ cup (80 mL) canned coconut milk or plant milk

¼ cup (20 g) cocoa powder

Pinch of salt

2¼ cups (200 g) quick-cooking oats

1 cup (85 g) unsweetened shredded coconut

1. Grease a baking sheet with oil.

2. In a bowl, whisk together the sugar, coconut oil, milk, cocoa powder, and salt. Add the oats and shredded coconut and mix well to combine.

3. Refrigerate the mixture for 15 minutes.

4. Use an ice-cream scoop to create 12 small balls of dough. Place the balls on the prepared sheet, leaving a bit of space between them, and refrigerate for 30 minutes.

5. Preheat the oven to 375°F (190°C).

6. Bake for 10 to 12 minutes. Let cool before serving.

Crème Brûlée

Serves 4 | **Prep Time: 15 min** | **Cook Time: 10 min** | **Rest Time: 30 min**

Here is proof that a classic can be improved without adjusting its special taste. Created in the 1600s—by an arsonist, probably—this creamy dessert can now be enjoyed by everyone, thanks to my vegan version of the recipe.

1 cup (200 g) cane sugar, divided
¼ cup (32 g) cornstarch
Pinch of turmeric
Pinch of salt
2 (14 oz/398 mL) cans coconut milk
4 teaspoons vanilla extract
2 teaspoons lemon juice
¼ cup (60 mL) vegan butter

1. In a saucepan, off the heat, combine ¾ cup (150 g) of the sugar with the cornstarch, turmeric, and salt.

2. Whisk in the coconut milk, vanilla extract, and lemon juice.

3. Set over medium-high heat and bring to a boil while whisking constantly. Lower the heat and simmer for 1 minute, then remove from the heat.

4. Add the vegan butter and stir until fully melted.

5. Divide the mixture between four ¾-cup (180 mL) ramekins. Refrigerate to cool completely.

6. Before serving, sprinkle with the remaining sugar, then quickly melt and caramelize the sugar by using a kitchen torch or by placing the ramekins under the broiler.

7. Serve immediately.

Carrot Cake

Makes 1 (9-inch/23 cm) cake | Prep Time: 30 min | Cook Time: 45 min | Rest Time: 20 min

Carrots are an excellent source of vitamins and nutrients. They taste great raw—the bunnies in your garden would agree—or cooked in savory dishes, and they make for delicious desserts, like this carrot cake. And I haven't even mentioned the frosting!

Cake:
- ½ cup (65 g) raisins
- 1½ cups (330 g) packed brown sugar
- ¾ cup (180 mL) plant milk
- ¾ cup (180 mL) vegetable oil
- ½ cup (125 mL) applesauce
- 1 teaspoon lemon juice
- 2 cups (220 g) grated carrots
- 2½ cups (310 g) all-purpose flour
- 1 teaspoon baking powder
- 1 teaspoon baking soda
- 1 teaspoon salt
- ½ teaspoon ground cinnamon

Frosting:
- 1 (2½ oz/75 g) block silken tofu
- 2 teaspoons lemon juice
- 1 teaspoon apple cider vinegar
- 1 tablespoon vegetable oil
- 1 teaspoon vanilla extract
- Pinch of salt
- 3 cups (360 g) powdered sugar

Chopped nuts, to decorate

For the Cake:

1. Preheat the oven to 350°F (180°C). Line a 9-inch (23 cm) cake pan with parchment paper.

2. Soak the raisins in boiling water for 5 minutes, then drain.

3. In a bowl, whisk or use a hand mixer to beat together the brown sugar, milk, oil, applesauce, and lemon juice. Fold in the grated carrots to incorporate. Set aside.

4. In a second bowl, whisk together the flour, baking powder, baking soda, salt, cinnamon, and soaked raisins.

5. Add the liquid ingredients to the dry ingredients and stir to combine.

6. Transfer the cake batter to the prepared cake pan.

7. Bake for 30 to 45 minutes or until a toothpick inserted into the center comes out clean.

8. Let the cake cool for 15 to 20 minutes before unmolding.

For the Frosting:

9. In a large bowl, add all of the ingredients and use a whisk or hand mixer to combine.

10. Add powdered sugar as needed to get a frosting consistency.

To Assemble:

11. Spread the frosting over the cooled cake. Decorate with nuts.

Upside-Down Pear Cake

Makes 1 (8-inch/20 cm) square cake | Prep Time: 30 min | Cook Time: 45 min

A word of advice: when visiting family, do not take this cake along and expect to leave with the leftovers, unless you intend to spark a family feud. Another tip: save the pear juice from the can and boil it in a saucepan, over medium-high heat, until reduced by half. Brush it on the cake right out of the oven. A delight!

1 tablespoon margarine or vegan butter, for pan

2 tablespoons granulated sugar, for pan

2¼ cups (280 g) all-purpose flour

1 cup (100 g) almond flour

1 cup (200 g) granulated sugar

2 teaspoons baking powder

1 teaspoon salt

1½ cups (375 mL) plant milk

½ cup (125 mL) vegetable oil

1 teaspoon vanilla extract

1 (28 oz/796 mL) can pear halves

8 maraschino cherries, halved

1. Preheat the oven to 350°F (180°C). Line an 8-inch (20 cm) square baking pan with parchment paper. Grease the parchment paper with vegan butter, then generously sprinkle with the 2 tablespoons sugar.

2. In a bowl, whisk together the all-purpose flour, almond flour, sugar, baking powder, and salt. Add the milk, oil, and vanilla extract. Beat until the batter is smooth. Set aside.

3. Drain the pears (save the juice to make pear syrup–see the recipe introduction). Place a maraschino cherry in the cavity of each pear half.

4. Set the pears side by side on the bottom of the baking pan, cherry side down.

5. Pour the cake batter over the pears. Bake for 45 minutes or until a toothpick inserted in the center of the cake comes out clean.

6. Let cool, and enjoy. The cake will keep in an airtight container in the fridge for up to 5 days.

Fruit Tart

Makes 1 (9-inch/23 cm) pie | Prep Time: 30 min | Cook Time: 30 min | Rest Time: 2 hours

This has been my favorite dessert since I was a kid! Thankfully, it's also a great way to get one's servings of fruit.

½ recipe Pie Pastry (page 175)

Pastry Cream:
½ cup (60 g) cornstarch
1 cup (200 g) granulated sugar
Pinch of salt
2 cups (500 mL) plant milk
2 cups (500 mL) soy cream
1 teaspoon vanilla extract
⅓ cup (80 mL) vegan butter

Fresh fruits (such as blueberries, raspberries, and stemmed and halved strawberries)
Fresh mint leaves, to garnish (optional)

1. Preheat the oven to 350°F (180°C).

2. Roll out the pie pastry. Line a 9-inch (23 cm) pie plate with the pastry. Prick the pastry with the tip of a fork in several spots, to prevent it from puffing up during baking.

3. Bake the pastry for 20 to 30 minutes. Meanwhile, make the pastry cream.

For the Pastry Cream:

4. In a saucepan, off the heat, combine the cornstarch with the sugar and the salt.

5. Whisk in the milk, soy cream, and vanilla extract. Set over medium heat and bring to a boil while whisking constantly.

6. Bring the pastry cream to a boil, lower the heat and keep cooking for 2 minutes while whisking constantly.

7. Remove from the heat and whisk in the vegan butter. Set aside.

8. Let the pastry cool for a few minutes once it's removed from the oven, then fill with the pastry cream.

9. Garnish with fresh fruits and refrigerate for 2 hours before serving.

Lemon Squares

Makes 9 squares | **Prep Time: 30 min** | **Cook Time: 5 min** | **Rest Time: 4 hours**

Life is severely lacking lemons. It's true! Everything today is white, purified, and sanitized. Whatever happened to the lemon-yellow color you used to see everywhere—from cars to plates to dresses and accessories? When will we ever see a lemon-yellow cell phone? Add some lemon to your life. Sure, you can make lemonade, but why not make these squares too?

Crust:
12 pitted Medjool dates
1 cup (150 g) whole almonds
2 tablespoons coconut oil
Pinch of salt

Filling:
½ cup (60 g) cornstarch
¾ cup (150 g) cane sugar
½ teaspoon turmeric
Pinch of salt
2 (14 oz/398 mL) cans coconut milk
¾ cup (180 mL) lemon juice
Zest from 2 lemons
1 (8 oz/225 g) block silken tofu

For the Crust:
1. In a food processor, blend all the ingredients together until the mixture has a uniform, crumbly texture.

2. Line an 8-inch (20 cm) square baking pan with parchment paper. Press the crust mixture into the pan and refrigerate for 2 hours.

For the Filling:
3. In a saucepan, off the heat, combine the cornstarch with the sugar, turmeric, and salt.

4. Whisk in the coconut milk, lemon juice, lemon zest, and silken tofu. Use an immersion blender to blend until smooth.

5. Bring the mixture to a boil while whisking constantly, lower the heat, simmer for 2 minutes, then remove from the heat.

6. Pour over the crust and refrigerate for 4 hours to set before cutting into squares.

ACKNOWLEDGMENTS

First of all, I wish to thank my wife, Amélie. Without her creativity, her sense of organization, and her moral support, this project would never have seen the light of day. I'm lucky to have such an exceptional woman in my life. I doubt my next wife will be as perfect.

Thank you to Antoine Ross Trempe and Emilie Villeneuve from Éditions Cardinal for their confidence and enthusiasm. Thank you to Jeannie Gravel and Daniel Raiche for their sense of aesthetics. Thank you to Alexandre Champagne, Samuel Joubert, and Dominique Lafond for their splendid photography. Thank you to Andréane Beaudin, Anabel Collin, Aurore Lehmann, Sophie Lyonnais, and Maude Delagrave.

Thank you to Emma Parry and Ali Lake. Thanks also to Robert McCullough, Katherine Stopa, Michelle Arbus, Andrew Roberts, Erin Cooper, Abdi Omer, and the rest of the Appetite and Penguin Random House Canada team. A special thanks to Rui Da Fonseca and Harry Rosen for the wonderful clothes, and to the Nüspace boutique for the furniture.

Thank you especially to all of you who follow me on social media, cook my recipes, and encourage me every day to keep going in light of your posts and comments. Please keep writing to me.

And lastly, thank you to my dog Wilson, who helps me clean the kitchen.

RECIPE INDEX

203